P9-CRM-585

PEAK PERFORMANCE
TRAINING
FOR BASKETBALL

Thomas Emma

©2003 Coaches Choice. All rights reserved. Printed in the United States.

No part of this book may be reproduced, stored in a retrieval system or transmitted, in any form by any means, electronic, mechanical, photocopying, recording, or otherwise, without the prior permission of Coaches Choice.

Throughout this book, the masculine shall be deemed to include the feminine, and vice versa.

ISBN: 1-58518-337-7
Library of Congress Control Number: 00-108314
Book layout: Deborah Oldenburg
Illustrations: Mariela Pophristova, James Connolly
Cover design: Jeanne Hamilton
Cover photo: Brian Bahr/Allsport

Coaches Choice
P.O. Box 1828
Monterey, CA 93942
www.coacheschoice.com

ACKNOWLEDGMENTS

I would like to thank all of my teammates (unfortunately a list too long to mention) and coaches (Mike Krzyzewski, Bill Foster, Fritz Mueller, Bruce Minerly, Arnie Sims, Chuck Swenson, Bob Wenzel, Steve Stienwedel, Terry Chili, and the late Ken Johnston Sr.) throughout the years, without whom this book could not have been written.

Special thanks to Jeanette Wai of Future Kids Computer Learning Centers for all her time and effort with the manuscript, and to James Connolly and Mariela Pophristova (illustrators) for their hard work and timeliness. I also want to thank Chip Engelland, president of Chip Shots, for his support and for sharing his basketball and promotional insight, and Matt White, strength and conditioning coach for the New York Athletic Club, for his help with the conditioning section of the book.

And finally, thanks to the game of basketball, where players are continually striving to reach their full potential.

To Paul:
I hope you and your family get some use out of this book.
Good Luck!
Tom G

PREFACE

During the planning of this book I kept one question constantly in mind: How do I bring the best product to the reader/basketball player/basketball coach? The answer came by looking at my own background and experience. Most of my young life was spent on the basketball court aspiring to improve and perfect my game. When I wasn't playing basketball, I was watching it, reading about it, or talking about it. In a nutshell, my existence revolved around the sport (some of you may be able to relate, I'm sure), and although it certainly was not the most balanced of lives, I was able to gain tremendous insight into the game and what it takes to reach your ultimate potential as a basketball player.

My other passion is strength and conditioning training. I started working to improve my strength and conditioning—as you may have already guessed—in order to elevate my basketball game. Throughout my high school playing career, I was constantly double and triple-teamed, regularly bumped and held by defenders, and every game generally became a battle of physical attrition between me and the opposing team. Because of this, I understood early on that if I was to survive and thrive in the game I loved, acquiring the highest level of physical conditioning my genetics would allow was a must.

Peak Performance Training for Basketball is created from a basketball player's perspective. The unique demands of the game were taken into consideration when designing the conditioning programs, and the special information and techniques detailed are specific to the sport of basketball. The overall goal of the book is to show you in a simple and easy to understand fashion how you can integrate strength and conditioning training successfully into a year-round basketball improvement program. I hope I achieved this goal.

Dedicate yourself to the concepts and training programs in *Peak Performance Training for Basketball* and anticipate becoming a better conditioned, more confident, and most important, an improved all-around basketball player.

CONTENTS

PART I: KEYS TO MAINTAINING PEAK PERFORMANCE

Warm-Up

Flexibility Training

Cool-Down

Injury Prevention

Components of Balanced Nutrition

Weight Control

Sample Meal Plans

PART II: BASKETBALL CONDITIONING

Energy Systems

Physical Fitness Basketball-Style

Basketball and Aerobic Training

Methods of Aerobic Exercise

Eight-week Aerobic Conditioning Program

Anaerobic Training for Basketball

Modes of Anaerobic Conditioning

PART III: STRENGTH TRAINING FOR BASKETBALL

Why Strength Train for Basketball?

Strength Training Basics

Strength Training Principles

Advanced Strength Training Methods

Improving Your Basketball Skills with Strength Training

INTRODUCTION

Not long ago strength and conditioning training for the majority of basketball players consisted of a month or so of long-distance jogging prior to the start of fall practice with perhaps a few pushups and sit-ups sprinkled in from time to time for good measure. And that is what the more dedicated players did! Others, including many at the professional level, engaged in little, if any, conditioning work during the off-season and basically "played" their way into shape once pre-season practice began.

My, how times have changed. Today coaches from junior high school to the NBA expect their athletes to come to training camp/pre-season practice in top condition. Playing your way into shape is definitely a thing of the past and is a sure ticket to "riding the bench" on opening night. A clear indication of the change in attitude toward strength and conditioning training in the basketball community is the addition of strength and conditioning coaches to NBA teams' payrolls. Some players even have personal trainers travel with them throughout the entire basketball season ensuring that they maintain optimal physical conditioning. Also, most college programs employ a basketball conditioning coach, or at least share a conditioning specialist with other sports teams on campus.

In order to find the central reason why strength and conditioning training have become necessities for basketball players, look no further than the game itself. Basketball has evolved from basically a non-contact finesse-oriented sport in the 1980s into a physical and fast-paced athletic endeavor in the 1990s. Fast break offense and pressure defense are in vogue in today's game, and body contact and rough play are the norm rather than the exception. Coaches at all levels of play are constantly searching for players who possess a combination of speed, strength, and athleticism, along with the requisite basketball skills. The days are long gone when an accurate jump shot and above-average ball handling ability assured success on the basketball court. Athletes must be physically strong, optimally conditioned, and dedicated to year-round preparation.

Peak Performance Training for Basketball is divided into four sections. Part One features strategies that will help you to maintain peak performance levels on a year-round basis. The topics include warm-up, cool-down, flexibility, injury prevention, along with an entire chapter on basketball nutrition.

Part Two deals exclusively with basketball conditioning. It starts with the basics (energy systems and general basketball fitness) and continues with detailed explanations of aerobic and anaerobic conditioning methods. Full-length sample aerobic and anaerobic training programs are included at the end of each section.

Part Three covers all aspects of strength training as it relates to basketball, including strength training basics and principles, advanced strength building methods, and exercise execution explanations and their corresponding illustrations for more than 35 movements. A year-round strength-training program, complete with sample routines for off-season, pre-season, and in-season cycles, is detailed at the end of the section (chapter 8).

Part Four introduces you to movement training for basketball. This section provides thorough descriptions of various techniques and drills (plyometric exercises, agility drills, jump rope methods, etc.) that will help you improve your jumping ability, explosiveness, and quickness. At the conclusion of the section (the appendix) is a year-round conditioning calendar that will assist players and coaches with workout scheduling.

PART I
KEYS TO MAINTAINING
PEAK PERFORMANCE

CHAPTER 1

Warm-Up, Flexibility Training, Cool-Down

Warm-Up

Regardless of what basketball/athletic-related activity (i.e. team practice, strength training, off-season plyometric work, agility drills, etc.) you're planning on engaging in, an organized and conscientious warm-up must be incorporated. Warming up correctly will contribute to productive workouts, enhanced performance, and, most importantly, help to prevent injury. Most college and all professional basketball teams put their players through an extensive and mandatory warm-up prior to each game and practice.

Preparing the body for intense all-out activity is a threefold undertaking. An overview of each phase of the warm-up process is explained in detail in Table 1-1.

Flexibility Training

Improving and maintaining flexibility is a must for any athlete and basketball players are no exception. Flexibility training will make you less susceptible to injury, while at the same time improving speed, agility, and explosive power. Flexibility work should be

Phase 1—Low Intensity Exercise

Perform five to eight minutes of light exercise, such as running in place, stationary biking, or slow-paced jogging. This exercise raises your body temperature and gets the blood flowing to your muscles, allowing you to stretch (Phase 2) through a greater range of motion.

Prepares the body for

Phase 2—Flexibility Routine

12 stretches (approximately 10 minutes, 30-50 seconds each)

Prepares the body for

Phase 3—Medium Intensity Involvement in Desired Activity

Examples: Strength training—two light, high-repetition (12-20) sets
Speed work—bounding, heel kicks, and strides (20-30 yards). Two sets.
Agility training—jumping rope at medium speed for three minutes. Two sets.

Prepares the body for

⇊

Intense All-out Activity

Table 1-1. The three-phase warm-up process for basketball players.

performed both before your conditioning workouts as a warm-up and afterward as a cool-down. Pre-workout stretching readies the body for strenuous exercise. Post-workout stretching is essential for recovery, as it helps with the removal of lactic acid (lactate), a substance that contributes to muscle soreness.

As with all conditioning disciplines, flexibility training requires full concentration. As you execute each individual stretch, be sure to maintain awareness of how the muscle feels. Work to the point of slight discomfort but never to the point of pain. As discussed in the section on warm-up techniques, it is advisable to do some light exercise for five to eight minutes prior to pre-workout flexibility training. Each individual stretch should be held for 20-50 seconds. This method of holding a stretch is called static stretching and is much safer and more effective than ballistic stretching where bouncing movements are used.

Two other modes of flexibility training have become relatively popular in recent years, especially among professional athletes. The first, passive partner stretching, entails, as the name implies, having a partner add light pressure to a stretch in order to increase joint and muscle range of motion. The other is known as proprioceptive neuromuscular facilitation (PNF) stretching, and involves a partner/facilitator leading an athlete through a series of stretching positions (contract, hold, relax, and movement) in 10-second intervals. Both techniques certainly have benefits if performed correctly and with the appropriate assisting personnel. Unfortunately, the majority of junior high school and high school programs do not have individuals on staff who are capable of teaching these techniques correctly and safely. Incorrect execution, especially when employing PNF stretching, can lead to injury. In light of this, players should use static stretching exclusively in their flexibility routines unless knowledgeable assisting personnel are available on a regular basis.

Flexibility Program

The following flexibility program details a stretching regimen that is tailor-made for a basketball player. The entire routine can be accomplished in 10 to 15 minutes, and it should be performed daily and on a year-round basis—off-days from practice in the regular season and off-season training breaks included. As you progress and become more flexible, you should feel free to add and subtract stretches as you see fit.

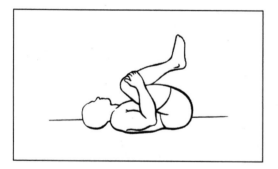 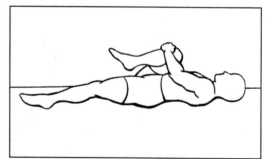

1. Knees to Chest

- Lie flat on your back with legs extended.
- Grasp your upper shins just below the kneecaps and pull your knees to your chest. Hold for 30 seconds.
- Alternate by pulling one leg at a time while keeping the other leg extended on the floor. Hold for 30 seconds.
- Perform two sets—one set with both legs and one set with alternating legs.

2. Back Arch

- Lie flat on your back with legs extended.
- Flex your knees, sliding your feet toward the buttocks, and lift your pelvis off the floor, arching your back.
- Perform one set. Hold for 45-60 seconds.

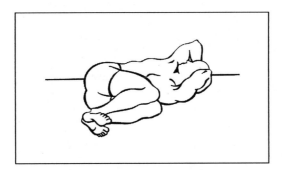

3. Hip Flexor Stretch

- Lie flat on your back with knees flexed and hands clasped behind your neck.
- Slowly lower both legs simultaneously to the floor, keeping your head, shoulders, and elbows flat on the floor. Hold at the bottom for 20 seconds.
- Perform two sets each side.

4. Lying Hamstring Stretch

- Lie flat on your back with your legs flexed and heels close to the buttocks.
- Extend one leg upward and grasp underneath it. Then slowly pull it toward you while keeping the other leg as straight as possible for 20 seconds.
- Perform two sets with each leg.

5. Reverse Plough

- Lie face down on the floor with your body extended.
- Place your palms on the floor between your chest and your hips.
- Press down evenly, and raise your head and trunk straight upward. Hold for 30 seconds.
- Perform two sets.

 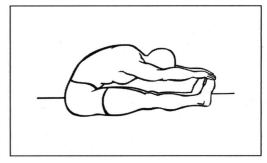

6. Plough to Hamstring Stretch

- Lie flat on your back with arms on your hips.
- Raise both slightly bent legs up over your head and slowly lower your feet to the floor.
- After holding the stretch for 20 seconds, return under control to the seated position with legs extended in front of you.
- Keeping both legs straight, bend forward at the waist and lower your trunk to your thighs, simultaneously stretching your hands to your toes. Hold for 20 seconds.
- Perform two sets.

7. Back/Quadriceps Stretch

- Lie face down on the floor with your body extended.
- Reach back and grab both ankles.
- Pull your ankles toward your upper back while at the same time lifting your chest off the floor.
- Perform one set. Hold for 45 seconds.

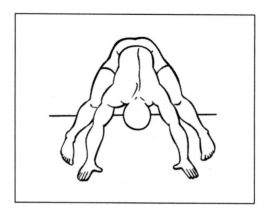

8. Standing Groin Stretch

- Stand with your legs spread approximately twice as wide as your shoulders.
- Bend straight down and attempt to touch your hands to the floor. Hold for 20 seconds.
- Perform two sets.

9. Standing Quadriceps Stretch

- Stand upright bracing yourself with one hand against a wall for balance.
- Reach down and grasp one foot (right hand/right foot, left hand/left foot).
- Pull your heel to your buttocks and hold for 20 seconds.
- Perform two sets with each leg.

10. Calf Stretch

- Stand upright with both hands against a wall and your arms fully extended.
- Lean forward, bending your arms and stretching your calves. Hold for 20 seconds.
- Perform two sets.

11. Shoulder Stretch

- Stand upright and cross one wrist over the other and interlock your hands.

- With arms extended behind your head, shrug your shoulder upwards and reach toward the ceiling. Hold for 30 seconds.
- Perform one set with your hands clasped each way.

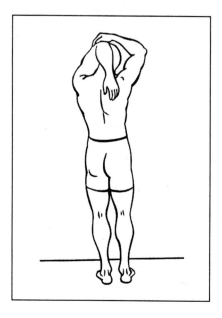

12. Triceps Stretch

- Sit or stand with one arm flexed and raised overhead next to your ear; rest your hand on your shoulder blade.
- Grasp your elbow with the opposite hand and pull it behind your head. Hold for 20 seconds.
- Perform two sets with each arm.

Cool-Down

Actively cooling down after intense exertion is extremely important and is a must for all basketball players. It will speed recovery and help clear lactic acid (lactate) from the system. Cooling down effectively will also help the body to return to its normal relaxed state faster, thus promoting physiological balance and sound sleep.

At the conclusion of each training session, you should engage in eight to ten minutes of some type of low-intensity activity; riding a stationary bike is ideal. Then perform an abbreviated stretching routine, focusing on the low back and hamstrings. After stretching, if the appropriate facilities are available, you should shoot some free throws and handle the basketball for five minutes or so. If you're cooling down after an upper-body strength training workout you may want to do some extra shooting and ball handling in order to loosen muscles and regain your feel for the basketball.

Injury Prevention

One of the most important, albeit the least exciting reasons to incorporate a year-round conditioning program is to prevent injuries. Basketball is a sport of quick, explosive movements, and often contact cannot be avoided. And remember, unlike football and hockey players, basketball players do not wear pads for protection. Despite these facts, along with the reality that the game itself is rougher and more physical than ever, the incidence of serious injuries has decreased significantly in recent years. The main reason is today's basketball players are superiorly conditioned compared to their predecessors.

By following the training programs and suggestions in this book, you can greatly reduce your risk of injury. Warming up and cooling down properly, increasing flexibility, and adhering to a balanced nutritional plan all contribute to preventing injury. Weight training consistently helps to strengthen connective tissues (ligaments and tendons) and increases bone density. Strong connective tissues make serious injuries such as the dreaded anterior cruciate ligament (ACL) tear in the knee less likely to occur. Increased bone density helps to prevent stress fractures and other impact related injuries. Enhanced physical conditioning also makes you less susceptible to an injury late in a game when the body is fatigued. And if you do sustain an injury, being in better shape will allow you to return to action quicker.

Before ending this section, a quick note on a common problem experienced by basketball players at all levels: low back pain. Discs in the back frequently become compressed from the hours upon hours most basketball players spend playing the game on concrete courts. This type of play can cause a condition called sciatica, which gives rise to pain extending from the lower back to the lower leg. Fortunately, there are ways to prevent low back problems before they arise. First, you should aspire to remain as flexible as possible, especially in the hamstrings. Second, you should maintain a reasonable body weight relative to your frame. Finally, and perhaps most importantly, you should develop strong abdominal and lower back muscles. Possessing strength in these areas can help relieve stress from the entire lower back region. Training your stomach and lower back muscles consistently, as suggested in this book, can greatly reduce the chances of low back injury.

CHAPTER 2

Basketball Nutrition

A well-balanced, nutritionally sound diet is essential for a hard training athlete. In order to consistently engage in strenuous workouts, you must have tremendous amounts of physical energy. The food you eat is the fuel from which this energy is derived.

There has been, and will continue to be, numerous theories as to the best diet for athletes. A strong argument can be made that athletes should keep their dietary intake simple without overdoing any particular aspect or becoming so strict in planning meals that they turn into a fanatic. Eating a balanced diet, one that includes plenty of water, a fair number of complex carbohydrates, sufficient protein, a fairly low intake of fat, and adequate vitamins and minerals, is recommended. The next section provides an overview of the various components of balanced nutrition, including nutritional percentages for carbohydrates, proteins, and fats.

Components of Balanced Nutrition

Water

Approximately two-thirds of your body mass is composed of water. It is without question the most important ingredient in any athlete's diet. Water performs many functions in the body, including lubricating joints, modulating body temperature (a key factor during vigorous exercise), carrying nutrients to cells and waste products away from cells, and helping with the digestion and absorption of food.

It is imperative that you drink at least eight 12-ounce glasses of water each day. When exercising on hot and humid days, up to 12 glasses should be consumed. Always make sure to keep your water intake high before, during, and after exercise sessions, as well as consistent throughout the day. Remaining optimally hydrated on a daily basis contributes to buoyant health and peak athletic performance.

Carbohydrates (% of total calories = 55% to 60%. Calories per gram = 4.)

Carbohydrates are the easiest form of food for the body to turn into energy. Complex carbohydrates, which include rice, potatoes, vegetables, beans, and pasta, should be the staples of your meal plan. These foods provide long-term energy and are easily digested. Simple carbohydrates, such as fruits and processed sugars, while easily digested, provide only short-term energy. With the exception of fresh fruit, it is a good idea to limit your consumption of simple carbohydrates. Complex carbohydrates should always be the primary part of your pre-game or pre-workout meal.

Proteins (% of total calories = 25% to 30%. Calories per gram = 4.)

Protein is used by the body to build and repair muscle tissue. Obviously, hard-training basketball players who are engaging in demanding activities such as weightlifting and plyometric training should include ample amounts of protein in their diet. The best sources of protein are eggs, fish, red meat, poultry, and dairy products. These foods are referred to as complete proteins, since they contain all the essential amino acids necessary to build muscle. Consuming approximately .50 to .60 grams of protein daily per pound of body weight should be sufficient for a basketball player.

Fats (% of total calories = 15% to 20%. Calories per gram = 9.)

Fats, similar to proteins and carbohydrates, are needed by the body. Fats supply the body with a major source of energy, protect vital organs, and help prevent starvation during a time of insufficient food intake. The problem is that the average American, including many athletes, derives up to 50% of his or her calories from fat. This amount of fat consumption not only adds unwanted weight to the physique, but can raise cholesterol levels, which increases the risk of heart disease. Make a conscious effort to stay away from fried foods, fatty meats, and high-fat diary products. In order to keep your fat intake low, try to get the majority of your protein from low-fat sources, such as fish, egg whites, skim milk, and poultry.

Vitamins

Although vitamins perform a variety of important functions, they are only needed by the body in small amounts. For example, vitamin D assists in the absorption of calcium and vitamin C enhances resistance to infection. Although vitamins are not a source of energy, they do release energy from the food you eat.

Two types of vitamin classifications exist: water-soluble (B and C) and fat-soluble (A, D, E, and K). Water-soluble vitamins are not stored in the body. Thus, extra amounts are flushed from the system easily. Fat-soluble vitamins, on the other hand, are stored in the body's fat and can be toxic if excessive amounts are consumed.

Minerals

More than 20 mineral elements are found in the body, 17 of which are necessary in your diet. Some of the most important minerals include calcium, copper, iodine, iron, magnesium, manganese, phosphorus, potassium, and zinc. Minerals help build strong bones, maintain bodily tissues, and help muscles work efficiently. Most of the minerals that your body requires can be obtained by eating a balanced diet.

Supplements

For a variety of reasons, not the least of which are attributed to the accomplishments of professional athletes (e.g., Mark McGuire smashing the 37-year-old major league baseball home-run record while using a variety of muscle-building supplements such as creatine and androstenedione—andro), the popularity of nutritional supplements has skyrocketed in the United States. Vast sums of money are being spent on these products annually, much of it by young athletes looking for that elusive competitive edge. In fact, the number of supplements that currently exist on the market is head-spinningly high. The unsubstantiated claims made by these supplements are relatively far-reaching to the point where most bases are covered, including weight gain, weight loss, increased energy, increased stamina, and even enhanced mental capacity.

Regarding supplements, most nutritional experts believe that if you're eating a nutritionally complete diet you can do without them. As a rule, the only supplement that most athletes should consume is one multivitamin per day, and if they have a sore throat or are on the verge of cold, they might also take a 1000-milligram tablet of vitamin C. Also, energy bars, such as the popular Power Bar® brand, can serve as a good pre-workout snack consumed 45 minutes or so before a training session. The other stuff, such as protein powders and so-called mega-mass tablets, are a waste of money, and are more likely to produce stomach cramps than added muscle growth. In fact, an extra helping of scrambled egg whites has been found to be just as effective as any of these supplements for building muscle and, with a little ketchup, tastes much better.

Alcohol, Drugs, and Tobacco

For a serious, hard-training athlete, staying clear of alcohol, drugs, and tobacco should be obvious. Unfortunately, in our complicated society, fraught with hard choices and peer pressure, it is not always so cut and dry. However, one thing is certain, using any of these substances, even on a casual basis, can lead to serious health problems and will hinder athletic performance substantially. Numerous well-known athletes, some from the ranks of the basketball arena, have short-circuited their careers due to their use of these products. So, do yourself and your game a favor, abstain from alcohol, drugs, and tobacco.

Weight Control

Basketball players have a variety of reasons for wanting to gain or lose weight. Some players need to increase their physical presence and power on the floor, thus adding weight and muscle is necessary. Others desire to lose weight in order to increase their speed, quickness, and stamina. In either case, athletes should work within their genetic makeup and body type (e.g., slim build, muscular build, heavy/large build, etc.) and maintain a reasonably low body-fat level – 6-to-12 percent for men and 12-to-18 percent for women. The next part of this chapter reviews several simple strategies for gaining and losing weight.

Weight Gain

In order to gain weight in a safe and efficient manner, you should focus on two major factors. First, you must take in more calories than you expend. For an average-size male, about 500 calories per day over what is burned off will be sufficient to gain approximately one pound of body weight a week. Such a gain is a safe amount provided it is lean body mass. Second, you should engage in a year-round strength training program, one that concentrates on building muscle weight by using basic exercises (bench press, squat, row) while performing low/medium repetition (i.e., 4-10) sets.

Always keep in mind that just because you're in a weight-gaining mode, you don't have carte blanche to eat anything and everything. Your fat consumption should remain relatively low. Gaining large amounts of body fat will inhibit your performance and may eventually cause health problems. Small amounts of extra protein can and should be consumed during a weight-gain cycle, but you should take care not to overdo it, as do many relatively well-intentioned young athletes who gorge themselves with protein daily in a futile attempt to gain massive amounts of muscle. The fact is that the body can only effectively metabolize some 30-to-35 grams of protein (approximately one-and-a-half small cans of tuna) at a given time. The best way to get maximum protein in your diet is to eat five or six small meals per day that are spaced three-to-four hours apart. Keep in mind that a weight-gain program should always be undertaken in the off-season.

Weight Loss

For basketball players who wish to lose weight, the first point to be conscious of is that the weight scale should never be the ultimate judge. The key factor in sound weight management is body composition (relative amounts of muscle, bone, and fat in the body). Overweight athletes should always make losing fat and gaining lean muscle tissue their number one dietary priority. Since muscle weighs more than fat, what you weigh is far less important than how it is distributed throughout the body. New Orleans Hornets point guard David Wesley stands six feet even and weighs 205 pounds. Although he is overweight by American medical standards, if you take one look at his lean, muscular physique, you quickly realize why body composition is the "name of the game." Your body composition level can be improved in a number of ways, including the following steps:

- Eat five to six small meals per day as opposed to the traditional three larger ones.
- Avoid eating heavy late at night before retiring—midnight snacks and late-night pizza binges are taboo.
- Eat high-fiber, low-fat meals as often as possible.
- Get the majority of your protein from low-fat sources such as egg whites, fish, lean meats, and poultry.
- Avoid fried foods, excess white breads, and simple carbohydrates with the exception of fresh fruits.
- Drink large amounts of water throughout the day.
- Engage in some form of aerobic exercise such as jogging or swimming for 20-to-60 minutes four-to-five days a week (off-season only).
- Stay current with your strength program. Building additional lean muscle mass helps the body burn fat more efficiently.
- Lose fat/weight gradually—no more than three-to-five pounds a week. Fad diets and quick weight-loss methods don't work.

Sample Meal Plans

Pre-Game Meal

When I played basketball competitively 15 years ago what constituted a pre-game meal was a 12-ounce steak (well-done), a baked potato (piled with sour cream), and if you were lucky, some type of vegetable. Well, at least it was partially right (the potato). Eating a high-protein, high-fat pre-game meal, as was the tradition in all sports for many years, is probably the worst thing you can do. Steak and other fatty meats are extremely hard to digest and can cause cramping and discomfort during a game. Fortunately, most knowledgeable coaches and trainers now realize that the customary "pre-game steak" was the wrong approach.

A pre-game meal should include ample portions of complex carbohydrates (i.e., pasta, rice, whole wheat pancakes, etc.), very little protein, and if possible, no fat. As mentioned earlier, carbohydrates are easily digested and, when broken down, produce glucose, which supplies the body's energy needs. Before intense physical exertion having large amounts of energy at your disposal is obviously crucial. Ample complex carbohydrates will do the trick. Pre-game meals should be planned three-and-a-half to four hours before tip-off.

Breakfast:	Two poached eggs Two slices of dry whole wheat or whole grain bread Medium-sized bowl of oatmeal with raisins Large glass of orange or fruit juice One 12-ounce glass of water
Lunch:	Large turkey sandwich on rye bread with lettuce and tomato Bowl of vegetable soup One 12-ounce glass of water
Snack:	Five whole wheat crackers with peanut butter Half of a banana One 12-ounce glass of water
Dinner:	Large piece of grilled salmon or halibut Baked potato with low-fat sour cream Large mixed salad with low-fat dressing Slice of pound cake One 12- ounce glass of water
P.M. Snack:	Small slice of whole wheat bread with cheese

Table 2-1. Sample daily meal plan for basketball players

Breakfast:	Six eggs, scrambled (two yolks only)
	Two dry slices of whole wheat or whole grain bread
	Medium-sized bowl of Raisin Bran (using 1/2 cup skim milk) and a sliced banana
	One large glass of grapefruit juice
	One 12-ounce glass of water
A.M. Snack:	Five saltine crackers spread with peanut butter
	Two 12-ounce glasses of water
Lunch:	Two broiled skinless chicken breasts
	Large serving of brown rice
	Medium serving of grilled vegetables
	One large glass of fruit juice
Midday Snack:	Serving of mixed nuts with dried fruit on top of low-fat yogurt
	One 12-ounce glass of water
Dinner:	Twelve-ounce cut of lean beef
	Baked potato with low-fat sour cream
	Large mixed salad with low-fat dressing
	One 12-ounce glass of water
P.M. Snack:	One slice of pound cake
	Large glass of skim milk with Ovaltine

Table 2-2. Sample daily weight-gain meal plan

Keep in mind the plans outlined in Tables 2-1 and 2-2 are meant to be a basic guide only. What dietary plan you should follow will depend on many factors, including your food tastes, individual metabolism, body size, and activity level.

PART II
BASKETBALL
CONDITIONING

CHAPTER 3

Basketball Conditioning Basics

Basketball is a sport of short, intense bursts of speed. During the course of a ball game, you are constantly starting, stopping, jumping, changing directions, and sprinting. Simply being in good physical condition—running five miles at a decent pace for example—is not enough for basketball players. In order to compete at peak levels, you must be in what many coaches and trainers like to call "basketball shape," the type of condition that allows you to go all-out for extended periods of time, recover quickly, and then proceed to go full-speed once again. Achieving this high degree of physical conditioning takes hard work and year-round dedication, along with a well-planned basketball-specific conditioning program. Your program must be progressive, including specified work:rest ratios and training protocols that relate to basketball, and it should take into account individual recovery requirements.

Energy Systems

Although the science of the body's energy systems is extremely complex (some would say boring as well), it is worthwhile that you have a fundamental understanding of how these systems affect the conditioning process. In this regard, perhaps the most important point to be aware of is that the energy released from the food you consume is utilized to manufacture a chemical compound called adenosine triphosphate or ATP. Muscle action is powered by the energy yielded from the hydrolysis of this compound.

ATP can be produced by three pathways. Two are considered anaerobic (without oxygen), the other aerobic (with oxygen).

The first pathway is called ATP-PC (phosphocreatine). PC, similar to ATP, is stored in the muscle and has an extremely high energy yield. The PC system itself is anaerobic, and the total amount of ATP that can be produced through this mechanism is finite. The ATP-PC pathway becomes involved when your muscles are giving maximal effort, such as sprinting 40 yards, performing a maximum weight lift, or jumping as high as possible to block a shot. The energy reserves from this system last only about ten seconds.

The second pathway capable of producing ATP is termed anaerobic glycolysis—frequently referred to as the lactic acid system. This system, as the name suggests, is anaerobic and does not involve oxygen. During glycolysis, carbohydrates (glycogen or glucose) are broken down to form ATP.

Anaerobic glycolysis takes over where the ATP-PC system leaves off, allowing you to extend high-intensity exercise. There are limits, however, as the buildup of lactic acid (lactate) triggers the commencement of fatigue (and the slowing of anaerobic glycolysis) usually within two and a half-to-three minutes after the start of vigorous work. In essence, this process forces you to discontinue exercising, or at least lower the intensity level considerably, in order to facilitate the removal of lactic acid from the body. For example, sprinting 800 meters or jumping rope "all-out" for three minutes would bring this system into play.

The final pathway in the energy production chain is the aerobic system. This system supplies the body with long-term energy and involves the use of oxygen. After two-and-a-half to three minutes of exercise, the body's ATP requirements are met mostly by the aerobic system. Unlike glycolysis, which can only use carbohydrates to free energy, the aerobic metabolism can break down both fats and proteins along with carbohydrates to produce ATP. Some popular forms of aerobic exercise include long-distance jogging, biking, and swimming.

It is important to note that the transition between energy pathways is not an instantaneous change but instead a gradual shift from one system to another. For example, when jumping rope intensely with a weighted jump rope for 35 seconds, energy comes from a combination of the ATP-PC system and the lactic acid system,

ATP-PC >>>>>> Anaerobic Glycolysis >>>>>> Aerobic System			
Time: 10 seconds >	3 minutes >	4 minutes >	30 minutes

Table 3-1. Energy pathway continuum

with glycolysis producing the majority of the necessary ATP. In another example, the energy for sprinting 440 yards would come mostly from anaerobic pathways (approximately 75 percent) with the balance (approximately 25 percent) coming from the aerobic system.

Physical Fitness Basketball-Style

As mentioned previously, basketball is a sport of explosive, fast-paced movements. Therefore, the demands of the game from a physiological standpoint are mostly anaerobic. The percentage breakdown, depending on your team's style of play (fast breaking, full-court pressing versus walk the ball up court, half-court defense etc.), is approximately 80 percent anaerobic and 20 percent aerobic. In order to be successful, you must tailor your conditioning routine accordingly. Keep in mind that because both aerobic and anaerobic maximums have much to do with genetics, you should work hard to reach your own personal potential without concerning yourself with the individual capacity of others for training.

CHAPTER 4

Aerobic Conditioning

Aerobic training is usually defined as any reasonably low-intensity (70 percent to 85 percent of your maximal heart rate) activity that is sustained for an extended period of time. Although some fitness professionals feel that aerobic benefits can be achieved in as little as 12 continuous minutes, for basketball purposes it is best to work within 20-minute to 45-minute time parameters.

In addition to total workout time, the intensity at which you exercise aerobically must be taken into account. The simplest way to measure the intensity of an aerobic activity is by using percentages of your maximum heart rate (max HR). Your estimated max HR can be easily figured by subtracting your age from 220. An 18-year-old athlete, for example, would have a max HR of 202 (220 − 18 = 202). After determining your max HR, you can then find your suggested aerobic training range. Most experts agree that to receive optimal aerobic benefits, you should train somewhere between 75 and 85 percent of your max HR. Using the example, 18-year-old athletes would need to elevate their heart rate between 151 and 172 beats per minute (bpm) in order to incur satisfactory aerobic training benefits. Of course, much would depend on the duration of the activity, the particular mode of exercise, and the genetic capacity of the individual.

Your heart rate can be conveniently calculated by using a heart rate monitor that is available for purchase at a relatively nominal cost at most fitness and sporting goods stores, or by simply checking your pulse rate by pinpointing your radial artery in the wrist and counting the number of beats for 10 seconds. Then, you can determine your heart rate (bpm) by multiplying the number of beats per 10 seconds by six.

Basketball and Aerobic Training

Through the years, considerable debate has swirled around the basketball conditioning community concerning a simple question: Where and how should aerobic training fit into a basketball player's year-round conditioning regime? Fifteen or twenty years ago, numerous well-meaning basketball coaches and trainers prescribed heavy aerobic work for their athletes throughout the off-season and pre-season. The conceptual basis of such a strategy was that conducting a high volume of cardiovascular exercise in the off-season would condition players' bodies to the extent where they could jump right into basketball workouts come time for them to engage in organized practice. This approach did have some merit, especially when you consider that it was the norm at the time for basketball players (including many professionals) to do very little in the way of physical conditioning in the off-season. Instead, players waited to play their way into shape during fall practice—a luxury most players don't have today by the way. It was, to a point, better than nothing. Current conventional wisdom, however, suggests that while basketball players should train consistently on a year-round basis, they should take care not to overindulge in aerobic training.

In recent years, the attitude toward aerobic exercise has changed significantly among many basketball conditioning experts. While it is still considered an important component of basketball conditioning, most experts agree that serious aerobic training should be limited to the early off-season (April to June), and be incorporated for no longer than six-to-eight weeks. Research (and in the author's case, firsthand experience) has shown that an excessive amount of aerobic work can inhibit jumping ability, explosive speed, and quickness, along with generally wearing down the body.

There are only three instances where you would extend your aerobic training beyond eight weeks: first, if an injury does not allow you to engage in basketball/anaerobic workouts; second, if, in order to improve on-court performance, you need to lose substantial amounts of body fat (exercising aerobically for more than 25 minutes contributes greatly to fat burning); and finally, if you are coming off a long layoff.

Remember, basketball is a sport of short, intense movements performed over and over and then over again; it is not a sport of slow, deliberate activity carried out in a continuous fashion. Therefore, the crux of your training should be of the anaerobic variety. Engaging in regular aerobic exercise early in the off-season will allow you to attain a conditioning base that can help prepare the body for subsequent anaerobic, basketball-specific workouts. In essence, aerobic training sets the stage for anaerobic training. Having a conditioned aerobic system also contributes to your ability to recover sufficiently during stoppages in play (e.g., foul shots, time outs, halftime, etc.).

An eight-week aerobic workout program is recommended for basketball players who begin working out early in the off-season, approximately four weeks after their campaign ends (sometime in mid-April to early May for most). The program, detailed later in the book, calls for five weeks of gradually building up your cardiovascular capacity, followed by one week of intensive aerobic work, and ending with two weeks of what is commonly referred to as "transition training", where you combine aerobic exercise with low-intensity anaerobic workouts.

Methods of Aerobic Exercise

Due to the popularity of aerobic exercise among the general public over the past 25 years, an almost endless number of options are at your disposal when it comes to training your cardiovascular system. Walk into any commercial health club these days, and you'll usually see an impressive array of aerobic exercise equipment, along with a full complement of offered aerobic and body conditioning classes. A wide variety of aerobic exercise equipment is also available for your home. And, if you're low-tech like me, there is always the old standby, long-distance running, where only a pair of running shoes and the wide-open spaces are required.

Whichever aerobic activities you chose (a half-dozen options are subsequently discussed in this section), make sure to follow the heart-rate parameters, which were previously discussed, and the duration and workouts per week recommendations outlined later in this chapter.

Long-distance Running

Long-distance running is the personal favorite aerobic activity of many individuals for a variety of reasons. First, it is inexpensive—all you need is a sturdy pair of running shoes and a little dedication. Second, because basketball is a running game, it stands to reason that in order to prepare physically for a basketball season, running should be your aerobic exercise of choice.

Third, in my own training, I have found long-distance running to be by far the most effective way to condition my aerobic system. Regardless of how much stationary biking or stair climbing I do in the gym, I just cannot seem to duplicate the physical condition I achieve from running long distances out on the road, along the beach, or around the track. Many of the basketball players with whom I work report this same experience.

Finally, and perhaps most important, is the fact that running outdoors on a nice spring day (the bulk of your aerobic work will generally be performed in the springtime) is not only extremely desirable for your lungs and legs, but for your head as well. Running along a scenic road, path, or beach engenders a sense of well-being unlike any other physical activity; not to mention this approach to aerobic conditioning offers a welcome change of pace after spending the better part of the past six months cooped up in a gymnasium.

As beneficial as long-distance running can be for your cardiovascular system, some drawbacks exist, however. For instance, if you have a history of impact-related injuries (chiefly bone spurs or shin splints), running long distances, especially on hard surfaces such as concrete or asphalt, can exacerbate these conditions.

In addition, basketball players who suffer from chronic low back pain should keep their long-distance running to a minimum, as should relatively bigger athletes (i.e., a 6'9", 250-pound forward), who because of their large body mass, can place tremendous strain on their tendons and ligaments from the constant pounding of foot fall after foot fall.

If you experience any of the aforementioned ailments, treadmill running may provide you with a viable alternative. Motorized treadmills usually have soft running surfaces and allow you to alternate speeds and grades easily, thus making workouts less stressful on the body.

Swimming

Regardless of your level of proficiency as a swimmer (most basketball players are not known for their water exploits), hitting the pool for a workout has many benefits. Swimming provides a fantastic full-body workout, as virtually every muscle in the arms, legs, and torso are involved to some degree or another. Along with furnishing a terrific cardiovascular training session, swimming regularly contributes to toning the physique and improving coordination. And the best news of all concerning water training is that whether you're swimming, running in the pool (a popular form of exercise in the sports community currently), or just treading water, it is extremely easy on your tendons, ligaments, and joints, offering perhaps the ultimate low-impact activity. Because of this, swimming/pool work is universally recognized as the most efficient way for injured athletes to maintain their level of conditioning during any downtime that they might have. Most professional sports teams (basketball included) have specially designed water-training programs for their injured athletes.

If your swimming skills are less than adequate, don't be discouraged: a plethora of accessories exist, such as kickboards and life vests, that will help keep you floating as you get your exercise. So, experiment with water training and give your body a well-deserved break from the pounding of the hard courts.

Stationary Biking

Riding a stationary bike has long been a popular form of aerobic exercise for athletes and non-athletes alike. With the exception of swimming/pool work, it is the most accepted form of exercise prescribed for injured athletes and for athletes returning from long layoffs. Stationary biking is low-impact, requires little in the way of expertise, and offers a method of exercising where the intensity can be easily regulated.

There are numerous types of stationary bikes currently on the market. They run the gamut from fancy, computerized models that gauge everything and anything (i.e., your heart rate, calories burned, revolutions per minute, etc.) to the simple hand-operated original that your father probably still has gathering dust in the attic. Regardless of what style you favor, the key to successful stationary bike workouts from an aerobic conditioning standpoint is to maintain your target heart rate throughout the exercise session. It is very easy to become lazy and lose your concentration on a stationary bike, especially when you're reading a magazine or watching television—two activities which you should avoid during your stationary bike workouts. Leave the leisurely training sessions to the businessmen and housewives at the gym and aspire to keep your attention on the task at hand: improving your cardiovascular condition.

Stationary biking exercises the large muscles of the lower body thoroughly and, unlike running or swimming, the resistance can be increased or decreased to suit your needs. Stationary bike workout classes have become popular at health clubs in recent years. In one class known as "spinning", the instructor leads the group through a fairly demanding interval-bike workout. You may want to experiment with this type of class from time to time during your aerobic training cycle.

Nordic Tracking

The Nordic Track is an exercise machine that simulates cross-country skiing. Other models exist, but the Nordic Track version is, by most experts' estimation, the best cross-country ski machine available. What in the world does cross-country skiing have to do with basketball you ask? Very little, but basketball players can, nevertheless, benefit by incorporating this exercise into their aerobic training programs. In fact, it is a widely held belief among exercise physiologists that elite Nordic skiers are the finest aerobically conditioned athletes (along with Tour De France cyclists and world-class rowers) in the world. Many of these athletes spend a good deal of time training on the Nordic Track.

The machine provides a terrific low-impact, cardiovascular workout that places negligible stress on your knees and lower back. It also affords the benefit of exercising your upper and lower body in unison. The only drawback to the Nordic Track is that it takes some getting used to, especially if you have no experience on skis. After a few sessions, however, the feeling of insecurity will usually diminish, and you'll be on your way to productive workouts. Most health clubs and fitness centers have some variation of a cross-country ski machine. The Nordic Track is, in my opinion, the best piece of aerobic equipment for your home—that is, if you can fit it through the front door.

Rowing

Elite rowers, similar to champion Nordic skiers, are among the best aerobically conditioned athletes in the world. They consistently score high on all varieties of cardiovascular fitness tests, and their training regimes are viewed by some as the most demanding in all competitive sports.

For most of you, rowing workouts will be performed indoors on a rowing machine. While rowing on a lake or river would be ideal, most basketball players have neither the time nor the inclination to perfect the skills necessary to row outdoors—not to mention the small stature to fit into a rowing shell without discomfort.

No matter where it takes place, rowing is an extraordinary exercise. It works all the major muscle groups in the body, and when performed at the appropriate intensity, allows for an excellent aerobic workout without impact or strain to connective tissues, joints, and muscles. Rowing machines are also relatively easy to use.

Two standard types of rowing machines are available at fitness clubs or on the market for purchase—hydraulic cylinder rowers and flywheel rowers. While both machines are adequate, many fitness professionals feel that the flywheel model simulates water rowing to a greater degree and places slightly less stress on the lower back region.

Before engaging in intense workouts on the rowing machine, it is imperative that you are thoroughly warmed up, because rowing is perhaps the most taxing of all aerobic activities. As a rule, basketball players with lower-back problems should abstain from rowing.

Stair Climbing

Working out on stair climbing machines was the rage of the fitness scene in the mid-late 1980s. It became the fashionable alternative to stationary biking at most gyms and health clubs. To this day, 20 years or so after its debut, stair climbing is still a very popular form of aerobic training.

In order to get the most out of your stair-climbing workouts, it is critical that you learn how to use the stair climber properly. Many athletes make the mistake of using the handlebars for support, either by grabbing them with their arms or leaning over them with their torso. Both actions undermine the effectiveness and intensity of a stair-climbing workout. As such, make sure and use the handlebars only to maintain balance and not to support your body weight.

Although stair climbing is basically a low-impact exercise, some risk of injury exists. Poorly made stair-climbing machines (unfortunately, there are many) can cause the knee to hyperextend dangerously. Also, some athletes complain of soreness in their hips after extended aerobic-training sessions on a mechanical stair-climbing machine. In my opinion, basketball players should use stair climbing as a supplement to other forms of aerobic training, but never as a major focus of their aerobic-conditioning efforts.

Eight-Week Aerobic-Conditioning Program

Table 4-1 illustrates a sample aerobic-conditioning program that should be performed from approximately mid-April to early-June, depending on when your season ends. Except for the extenuating circumstances previously mentioned, your aerobic training should be discontinued by the end of June at the latest.

Week 1:	Monday	20 minutes	Friday	22 minutes
Week 2:	Sunday	24 minutes	Friday	26 minutes
	Tuesday	25 minutes		
Week 3:	Sunday	28 minutes	Friday	30 minutes
	Tuesday	30 minutes		
Week 4:	Sunday	32 minutes	Saturday	34 minutes
	Tuesday	34 minutes		
Week 5:	Monday	35 minutes	Thursday	36 minutes
	Wednesday	36 minutes	Saturday	38 minutes
Week 6:	Monday	40 minutes	Thursday	45 minutes
	Tuesday	42 minutes	Saturday	45 minutes
Week 7:	Tuesday	35 minutes/low-intensity anaerobic workout		
	Friday	30 minutes/low-intensity anaerobic workout		
Week 8:	Tuesday	32 minutes/low-intensity anaerobic workout		
	Friday	30 minutes/low-intensity anaerobic workout		

Table 4-1. A sample eight-week aerobic-conditioning program.

CHAPTER 5

Anaerobic Conditioning

Physical activity is considered "anaerobic" when you are exercising at about 85 to 100 percent of your maximum heart rate. The following instances are examples where basketball players work anaerobically during competition: sprinting back on defense after a change of possession, dribbling the basketball up the floor against man-to-man, full-court pressure defense, and when constantly jumping and landing while battling for a rebound.

The key to successful anaerobic conditioning is to work as hard as possible for the prescribed time and/or distance. As discussed previously, the high intensity of anaerobic training will only allow you to exercise in short bouts, three minutes or so being the maximum, before fatigue gets the best of you. Unlike aerobic activity, little need exists to monitor your heart rate during anaerobic training sessions, as the pain in your lungs and legs will let you know quickly if you're in your "anaerobic training zone."

Anaerobic Training for Basketball

In other anaerobic sports, participants, such as football players or short-distance sprinters, are exclusively concerned with the front end of the anaerobic time spectrum (the average football play lasts less than eight seconds and world-class sprinters cover 100 meters in less than 10 seconds). Basketball players, however, must condition their anaerobic systems to allow for intense split-second movements (i.e., diving for a loose ball); as well as long stretches of hard running that may take place when they're involved in a fast-paced, transition game with minimal stoppages in play.

Anaerobic training is difficult. In fact, it can be flat-out painful. As a rule, it is, by far, the most abhorred aspect of physical conditioning among basketball players. Notwithstanding, it is a necessary evil of basketball conditioning and must be approached in an organized, progressive manner.

The anaerobic training program that I recommend lasts for 14 weeks, beginning in mid-June and ending about four weeks prior to the start of fall practice (refer to Table 5-1). This program includes a two-week transition period from aerobic training, seven weeks of strides and sprints on the track, one rest week, and culminates with four weeks of on-court sprints, combined with stadium step running and/or hill running (note: if stadium steps or hills are not accessible, track work can be substituted).

Anaerobic conditioning sessions should be accomplished two days per week in the off-season. It is recommended that you perform your anaerobic workouts on separate days from your agility and plyometric training. With rare exception, all three disciplines combined into a single day of training would be too taxing on your body. This approach will also discourage overtraining. In the event you participate in numerous, relatively intense full-court games (summer league or pick-up) throughout the off-season, you may want to trim your anaerobic workouts down to one per week from time to time, especially if you begin to feel fatigued. On the other hand, if you engage in little full-court scrimmaging during the summer, it is recommended that you add a third anaerobic workout to your week.

Work:Rest Ratios

When designing anaerobic conditioning programs for basketball, it is critical that basketball-specific work:rest ratios are incorporated. The work:rest ratio denotes the work period of an activity relative to the rest period. For example, if you sprint for 50 seconds and then rest for 100 seconds before sprinting again, your work:rest ratio would be 1:2.

Depending on your team's style of play and your position, basketball typically involves a work:rest ratio of approximately 1:1 to 1:3. In order to reach peak levels of conditioning and performance, you must train your anaerobic systems in accordance with these percentages.

Typically, the longer the bout of anaerobic activity, the smaller the work:rest ratio. For instance, jumping rope with a heavy-handled rope for three minutes requires a work:rest ratio of 1:1. At the other end of the anaerobic time spectrum, sprinting for 30 seconds or less would require a work:rest ratio of 1:3.

Week	Day	Workout	Reps/Distance	Rest Periods
#1	Tuesday	Stride	2 x 400	3 minutes
	Friday	Stride	3 x 400	3 minutes
#2	Wednesday	Stride	3 x 400	3 minutes
	Saturday	Stride	4 x 400	3 minutes
#3	Tuesday	Stride	4 x 400	3 minutes
		Stride	2 x 300	2.5 minutes
	Friday	Stride	4 x 300	2.5 minutes
		Stride	4 x 200	1.5 minutes
#4	Wednesday	Stride	2 x 300	2.5 minutes
		Stride	6 x 200	1.5 minutes
	Saturday	Stride	1 x 300	2.5 minutes
		Stride	8 x 200	1.5 minutes
#5	Tuesday	Stride	8 x 200	1.5 minutes
		Stride	4 x 150	1.25 minutes
	Friday	Stride	6 x 200	1.5 minutes
		Stride	2 x 150	1.25 minutes
		Stride	4 x 100	45 seconds
#6	Wednesday	Stride	6 x 200	1.25 minutes
		Sprint	4 x 100	45 seconds
		Stride	2 x 150	1 minute
	Saturday	Stride	4 x 200	1.25 minutes
		Sprint	4 x 100	45 seconds
		Sprint	4 x 80	40 seconds
#7	Tuesday	Stride	2 x 150	1 minute
		Sprint	2 x 100	45 seconds
		Sprint	6 x 80	40 seconds
	Friday	Stride	4 x 100	30 seconds
		Sprint	4 x 80	30 seconds
		Sprint	2 x 60	30 seconds

Table 5-1. Recommended 14-week anaerobic conditioning program

NOTE: Distances listed are in meters. Rest intervals are prescribed with elite, highly conditioned athletes in mind. Depending on the player's level of conditioning, rest periods between sprints can be extended 10 to 15 seconds. Sets take the place of distances for court drills.

Week	Day	Workout	Reps/Distance	Rest Periods
#8	Wednesday	Stride	3 x 100	30 seconds
		Sprint	4 x 80	30 seconds
		Sprint	6 x 40	30 seconds
	Saturday	Stride	2 x 100	30 seconds
		Sprint	6 x 60	30 seconds
		Sprint	2 x 40	30 seconds
#9	Tuesday	Stride	2 x 100	30 seconds
		Sprint	2 x 60	30 seconds
		Sprint	4 x 40	30 seconds
		Sprint	4 x 20	25 seconds
		Sprint	4 x 10	20 seconds
	Friday	Stride	2 x 100	30 seconds
		Sprint	2 x 60	25 seconds
		Sprint	2 x 40	25 seconds
		Sprint	2 x 20	25 seconds
		Sprint	6 x 10	20 seconds
		Sprint	2 x 40	25 seconds
		Sprint	2 x 50	25 seconds
#10		Rest Week		
#11	Wednesday	Stride	2 x 100	30 seconds
		Uphill Sprint	2 x 60	40 seconds
		Uphill Sprint	4 x 40	30 seconds
		Uphill Sprint	2 x 20	25 seconds
		Uphill Sprint	4 x 10	20 seconds
		Uphill Sprint	2 x 60	40 seconds
	Saturday	Court-Length Stride	4 times	30 seconds
		Breadth Sprint	2 sets	3 minutes
		Suicide	4 sets	1 minute
		Diagonal Sprint	2 sets	1 minute
		L Sprint	1 set	1.25 minutes

Table 5-1 (continued). Recommended 14-week anaerobic conditioning program

NOTE: Distances listed are in meters. Rest intervals are prescribed with elite, highly conditioned athletes in mind. Depending on the player's level of conditioning, rest periods between sprints can be extended 10 to 15 seconds. Sets take the place of distances for court drills.

Week	Day	Workout	Reps/Distance	Rest Periods
#12	Tuesday	Stride	2 x 100	30 seconds
		Stadium Steps	2 x 60	40 seconds
		Stadium Steps	4 x 40	30 seconds
		Stadium Steps	4 x 20	25 seconds
		Stadium Steps	2 x 10	20 seconds
		Stadium Steps	2 x 60	40 seconds
	Friday	Court-Length Stride	4 times	30 seconds
		Half-Dozens	2 sets	1.25 minutes
		L Sprint	3 sets	1.25 minutes
		Suicide	4 sets	1 minute
		Breadth Sprint	1 set	2.5 minutes
#13	Wednesday	Stride	2 x 80	30 seconds
		Uphill Sprint	4 x 40	30 seconds
		Uphill Sprint	2 x 20	25 seconds
		Stadium Steps	4 x 40	30 seconds
		Stadium Steps	2 x 20	25 seconds
	Saturday	Court-Length Stride	4 times	30 seconds
		Diagonal Sprint	4 sets	1 minute
		Suicide	2 sets	1 minute
		Half-Dozens	4 sets	1 minute
		L Sprint	2 sets	1.25 minutes
#14	Tuesday	Court Length Stride	4 times	30 seconds
		Breadth Sprint	2 sets	2.5 minutes
		Diagonal Sprint	4 sets	1 minute
		Half-Dozens	4 sets	1 minute
		Suicide	4 sets	1 minute
	Friday	Court-Length Stride	4 times	30 seconds
		Half-Dozens	2 sets	1 minute
		Suicide	4 sets	minute
		Diagonal Sprint	4 sets	1 minute
		L Sprint	4 sets	1 minute
		Breadth Sprint	2 sets	2 minutes

Table 5-1 (continued). Recommended 14-week anaerobic conditioning program

NOTE: Distances listed are in meters. Rest intervals are prescribed with elite, highly conditioned athletes in mind. Depending on the player's level of conditioning, rest periods between sprints can be extended 10 to 15 seconds. Sets take the place of distances for court drills.

The chart presented in Table 5-2 summarizes the various durations for anaerobic training and the appropriate work:rest ratios involved.

Work/Time in Seconds	Work:Rest Ratios
0 to 45	1:3
45 to 120	1:2 to 1:1
120 to 180	1:1

Table 5-2. Anaerobic exercise times and work:rest ratios.

Modes of Anaerobic Conditioning

The most efficient way to condition your anaerobic systems for basketball is to run. After all, running is the essence of the sport, and every basketball player, regardless of position or talent level, must have the ability to run up and down the floor. Therefore, the bulk of your anaerobic training will consist of strides and sprints on the track and sprints on the court, supplemented with stadium-step and uphill running. A limited number of additional options, including jumping rope with a weighted rope and interval stationary bike training, can be employed in place of running from time to time, but track and court running workouts should always be your priority.

Strides

Stride workouts provide a good transition from your aerobic training sessions. They involve reasonably high-exertion runs, where your concentration is on proper running form rather than on reaching maximal speed. For the most part, strides are used when running medium distances (100 to 800 meters).

Sprints

Sprints are full-speed, short-duration efforts (100 meters or less); they are best incorporated after four weeks or so of stride work. Sprinting can also be performed by running up hills or stadium steps to add variety to your workouts (refer to chapter 11).

Court Sprints

Most basketball players are familiar with court sprints, such as the dreaded suicide drill. The final four weeks of your anaerobic conditioning cycle will consist mostly of on-court sprints, including suicides (sorry). This approach should have you in peak form and ready to go by the first day of fall practice.

☐ Drill: Suicide

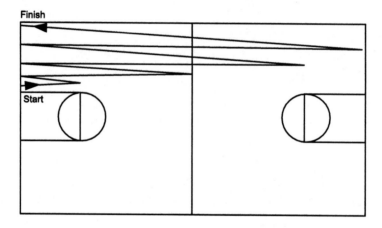

Execution: Beginning on one baseline, sprint to the adjacent foul line and back to the baseline; then sprint to the half-court and back to the baseline; then sprint to the far foul line and back to the baseline; and end by sprinting to the opposite baseline and back to the starting point.

☐ Drill: One-Minute Breadth Sprint

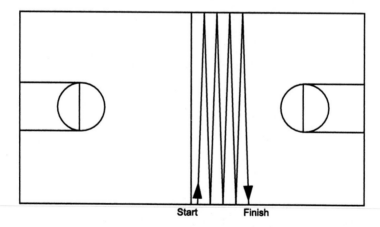

Execution: Begin on one sideline and sprint to the opposite sideline and back. Continue for one minute without stopping.

☐   Drill: Diagonal Court Sprint

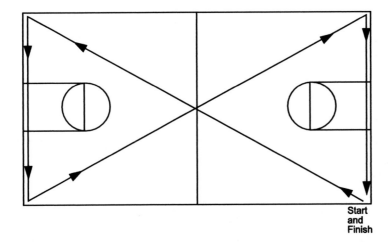

Execution: Facing across the full length of the court, begin where the left sideline joins with the baseline. Sprint diagonally across the court to the opposite sideline/baseline intersection, turn left, and then sprint along the baseline to the adjacent sideline/baseline intersection. Continue by turning to your left and sprinting diagonally across the court once again to the far side sideline/baseline intersection. Finish by turning to your right and sprinting along the baseline to the starting point.

☐   Drill: Half Dozens

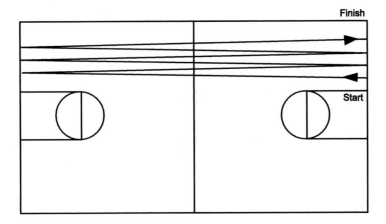

Execution: Begin on one baseline, and sprint to the opposite baseline and back. Repeat six court-length sprints without stopping.

☐   Drill: 35-second L Sprint

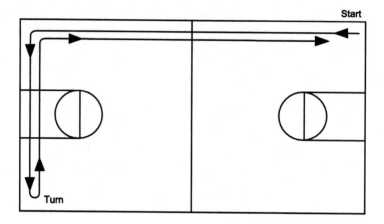

Execution: Begin on any sideline/baseline intersection. Sprint the length of the court along the sideline, turn 90 degrees at the end line, and then sprint the baseline to the opposite corner. Proceed by turning 180 degrees and retracing the run, starting with sprinting the baseline and finishing by sprinting the sideline to the starting point. Repeat as many times as you can in 35 seconds.

PART III
STRENGTH TRAINING
FOR BASKETBALL

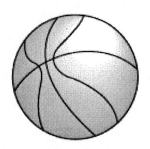

CHAPTER 6

Basketball Strength Training Basics and Beyond

Why Strength Train for Basketball?

During the past decade and a half, the sport of basketball has gained in popularity many times over. More people are playing and watching basketball than ever before. Because of this skyrocketing level of interest, the game has become intensely competitive at all levels. As a result, in order to excel in the current competitive climate, players must do everything humanly possible to reach their full potential.

What Strength Training Can Do for You

Strength training has many by-products that can enhance your performance on the basketball court. For example, you will become more explosive and powerful in your movements, whether you are driving to the hoop or lunging for a rebound. Your ability to absorb contact will also be improved, thus you will be less likely to be knocked off balance while shooting, fighting for position in the post, or handling the ball on the perimeter. You will set better, more solid screens on offense, and fight through picks more forcefully on defense. Your speed and quickness will improve, especially that all-important first step. You will find yourself jumping higher and getting off the floor quicker. Your grip will strengthen substantially, and rarely will opponents knock the basketball out of your hands once you've established possession. In addition, the stronger you are, the better your stamina and endurance will be. This will enable you to perform effectively during the last few minutes of a game and at the end of a long, grueling basketball season.

Training with weights also helps prevent injuries, prolong your career, and rehabilitate yourself from an injury. And as a direct result of lifting weights and becoming stronger, your confidence in yourself and your game will increase. Pumping iron promotes team camaraderie as well. The weight room is a place where players can work out in a congenial atmosphere, away from the critical eye of coaches. Teammates can encourage one another to test their physical limits. In the process, they become generally closer as a ball club. Furthermore, if a player wants to add weight to his physique, the best way to accomplish this goal is to combine strength training with a high-calorie diet. In addition, if you want to lose pounds, training with weights increases your metabolic rate, a factor that allows you to burn fat more efficiently. While there are plenty of other benefits you will achieve by strength training, the aforementioned should be more than enough to convince you to hit the weights.

Misconceptions Concerning Lifting Weights and Basketball Players

Misconceptions abound regarding the use of weight training as a conditioning tool for basketball. Although there are still some critics, most coaches and fitness professionals fully realize how important strength training is to a basketball player's success.

Some of the more common misconceptions associated with strength training and basketball include the following:

▸ *Lifting weights will adversely affect shooting touch.* Lifting weights will not hinder shooting touch provided you continue to practice shooting skills. In fact, your shooting will improve with strength training. As you become stronger, your shooting range will increase, you will shoot more accurately while absorbing contact, and your shooting percentage from both the field and the free-throw line will improve, particularly late in a game when fatigue sets in.

▸ *Weight training will lessen flexibility.* Involving yourself in a properly planned strength training program will not reduce your level of flexibility if you perform the exercises correctly and through a full range of motion. Recent research appears to show lifting weights can actually increase flexibility to some extent. Of course, you should incorporate a stretching routine as part of your overall-conditioning program.

▸ *Lifting weights will add unwanted bulk.* It is extremely difficult to gain tremendous amounts of lean body mass without chemical assistance, such as anabolic steroids. And if you take into account all the other physical activities basketball players are involved in outside the weight room (e.g., playing ball, running, etc.), it is virtually impossible to become too bulked up. Just take a look at some of the top NBA players who lift weights regularly, like Ben Wallace, Steve Francis, and Wally Szczerbiak, and you will see they all have good muscle size, definition, and tone, while not being overbulked.

▸ *Lifting weights will slow you down.* As mentioned earlier, training with weights will improve your strength and explosiveness, which results in being able to run faster, not slower. Take one look at the powerful bodies of world-class sprinters and you'll see that strength enhances speed.

▸ *Women basketball players should not lift weights.* On the contrary, women ballplayers should not only strength train; but basically use the same routines as their male counterparts. When it comes to strength training, a basketball player is a basketball player, regardless of gender.

▸ *Players at different positions should train differently.* Basketball players at all positions from point guards to power forwards, should strength train similarly. Physical differences must be respected, however. For example, taller players may have trouble performing deep squats because of the length of their legs.

▸ *Basketball players should not lift weights during the season.* This myth could not be further from the truth. Lifting weights during the season is every bit as important, if not more so, than in the off-season. Maintaining the strength you have built in the off-season and pre-season is absolutely crucial to your success.

One Last Point

One point worth emphasizing before additional information on strength training for basketball is covered is that you are a basketball player first and foremost, and strength training, while important, should be used as a supplement to your on-court work. Your goal is not to become an Olympic weightlifter or a bodybuilding champion. All the weight training in the world will mean nothing to your performance in-between the lines unless you diligently work on your game. Skill development comes first; strength and conditioning are an important second. Always remember that working out with weights is a great way to gain an edge on the competition. Just keep it in perspective.

Strength Training Basics

Before beginning your strength training program, you must first become familiar with the basics aspects of working out with weights. The following information can help get you started on the right track.

Weight Training Equipment

There are basically two types of weight training equipment you will be using: free weights (accompanied by exercise benches and power racks), and a variety of weight machines. Most gyms have a full complement of each type. Free-weight equipment consists of barbells and dumbbells. A good exercise bench should be sturdy and adjustable, allowing for different incline positions. Power racks are used for squatting and other heavy standing movements (e.g., upright rows, push presses, barbell shrugs, etc.). A substantial number and variety of strength training machines are currently available in the market. The most useful are the lat pull-down, leg press, cable row, leg extension, leg curl, and pullover machine.

Attire

☐ *Clothing:* Loose, comfortable clothing is best for strength training. What you wear on the basketball court is fine. The most important thing is that your clothing does not hinder your movement and exercise performance. In a cold gym, it is suggested you wear some type of sweatsuit, at least until your body warms up.

☐ *Shoes:* Some shoes exist that have been designed specifically for weightlifting, but they are not necessary. Most basketball sneakers and cross-training shoes are suitable. Running or jogging shoes lack lateral support and should be avoided.

☐ *Gloves:* Weightlifting gloves are optional. Some individuals who lift weights feel that such gloves provide you with a better grip. Gloves can also help prevent calluses from developing on your hands.

☐ *Weightlifting belt:* A weightlifting belt is typically four to six inches wide and made of nylon or leather. The belt is designed to support the lower back during heavy lifts. Although some trainers feel weight belts are not necessary, and that their benefit is mostly psychological, personally I suggest that you wear one while working out, especially when performing heavy standing exercises.

☐ *Straps:* Straps are used mostly by bodybuilders to prevent grip fatigue during exercises, such as chin-ups and upright rows.

☐ *Waist harness/weighted vest:* Both of these pieces of equipment allow you to add weight to your frame in order to increase the intensity of your workout when you are performing body-weight exercises (e.g., chin-ups, dips, etc.).

Safety

☐ *Warm-up:* If you hope to reduce your chances of being injured and have productive strength workouts, you must be sufficiently warmed up. Warming up prior to a strength training session is a three-fold process. First, prepare your muscles for stretching by doing some light exercise, such as riding a stationary bike, jogging, running in place, or jumping rope for five to eight minutes. Second, perform the flexibility program that was previously discussed in the first chapter of this book. Finally, warm up the specific muscle groups you will be training. This means that the first set or two of an exercise you perform should be executed with light-to-moderate weight, for a relatively high number of repetitions. Following these guidelines will enable your joints, tendons, and muscles to loosen gradually and become prepared for the heavier resistance to come later in the workout.

☐ *Spotters:* It is essential that you use a spotter when performing heavy sets of bench presses, incline presses, shoulder presses, and squats. Neglecting this factor can result in serious injury. In addition to ensuring your safety, an attentive, knowledgeable spotter can correct errors in your lifting form and help you get the most out of a set by giving just enough assistance to enable you to complete that final repetition.

☐ *Heavy singles:* Many strength training-related injuries would be prevented if one-repetition lifts were avoided. Besides trying to impress your friends in the gym, absolutely no reason exists to perform singles. Three- or four-repetition sets are far superior to maximum-weight singles for building strength and muscle.

☐ *Collars:* It is important that you get in the habit of using collars on the bars on all barbell exercises. They will ensure that weight plates do not slide and cause you to lose control of the bar.

☐ *Check equipment:* All equipment should be checked for safety before use. For example, make sure that benches are sturdy, plates are tight to the bar, machine cables are not worn, and collars are secure. Also, be aware of what is going on around you, especially in a crowded weight room.

☐ *Be conscious of fatigue and minor discomfort:* If you feel overly tired or encounter minor discomfort in your muscles, tendons, or joints, stop training immediately. Although it may be possible to continue with your workout, it is best to play it safe and come back to train another day. Heeding this simple advice can prevent many injuries.

Strength Training Principles

☐ *Sets and repetitions:* Sets and repetitions are the units of measure used in strength training. For example, pressing a pair of dumbbells overhead eight consecutive times with only a brief pause in-between lifts constitutes one set of eight repetitions. The simple notation used to denote such a performance is 1 x 8. The first number listed always represents sets, and the second number represents repetitions.

☐ *Pyramid sets:* For the most effective results from your strength training efforts, it is recommended that you pyramid your training. As the term suggests, pyramiding entails progressing from lighter weight sets to your heaviest set and then lowering the resistance on your last set or two. The notation would look something like this: 1 x 15, 1 x 10, 1 x 6, 1 x 8, 1 x 10. Training in this manner will help ensure maximum muscle fatigue and strength gains.

□ *Multi-joint exercises:* Multi-joint exercises work more than one muscle group at a time. An example of a multi-joint exercise is the incline press, which exercises the upper chest, front deltoids, and the triceps. These types of movements will be the core of your strength training program.

□ *Single-joint exercises:* Sometimes referred to as auxiliary exercises, single-joint movements work one muscle group at a time. Two examples of single-joint exercises are dumbbell flies for the chest and barbell curls for the biceps. These kinds of exercises will supplement the multi-joint movements that you perform in your training. Because you will be exercising a small, isolated mass of muscle, no less than six repetitions per set of a single-joint exercise should be performed.

□ *Train the largest muscle groups first:* It is important that you train your muscles from largest to smallest. Two basic reasons exist for this ordering of exercises. First, the smaller muscle is already the weak link in the strength chain when executing any multi-joint exercise. In the bench press, for example, training the triceps before bench pressing would further weaken the smaller muscle (triceps), thus limiting the workload for the muscle you are attempting to exercise (chest). Second, the bigger the body part, the more energy it takes to train. Because your energy levels are higher at the beginning of a workout, it is best to exercise larger muscle groups (hips, legs, back, etc.) first in your weight-training sessions.

□ *Strength progression:* The major premise of sound strength training is obviously strength progression. To encourage this, it is best to perform the majority of your sets (not including your warm-up sets) to or near the point of muscular failure. For example, if your program calls for an 8-repetition set, you would choose a weight that would allow you to complete eight repetitions and no more. When more than eight repetitions can be executed in good form, it is time to add weight. Usually a 5% increase is sufficient for multi-joint exercises. With most single-joint movements, weight increases will be less frequent, and the emphasis should be on working the muscle through the full range of motion in a controlled manner. Of course, finding the appropriate resistance level for each of the exercises in your program will take some time and a period of trial and error, especially if you are a novice or coming off a long layoff. Keep in mind that strength progression usually comes quickly for beginners. In fact, you can expect to experience substantial gains in strength during your first two months or so of training. Unfortunately, as time goes on, and your body adjusts to the new stress being placed upon it, increases in strength become more difficult. Progression is still possible, however, albeit at a slower pace, and should continue to be the priority.

□ *Breathing:* Typically, you will find it easier to inhale during the lowering phase of the exercise and to breathe out during the lifting or work part of the movement. Personally, I have found when training with weights my breathing tends to regulate naturally without much thought. Obviously, you should never hold your breath when lifting weights.

□ *Rest:* A counselor at a five-star basketball camp once said to me, "If you want to soar with the eagles in the daytime, you can't hoot with owls at night." Sound advice. As a hard-training athlete, you must get adequate sleep and rest. Sleep requirements vary from person to person. Some people are able to get by on only five or six hours a night, while others require eight to ten hours. Most active basketball players involved in a strength training program will need at least eight hours of sleep per night. Young ballplayers (i.e., thirteen to eighteen) will usually require more sleep than their older counterparts. As with strength training, you should stay in tune with your body's needs and act accordingly.

Besides sleeping, it is also imperative that you rest your body and not wear yourself down with too many activities outside of basketball. For example, if you're competing in three mountain biking races weekly and water skiing five hours a day on weekends during your pre-season conditioning cycle, you are probably doing too much. While no one wants to ruin your summer fun, you must keep your outside pursuits at reasonable levels if you hope to be strong and in peak condition for the basketball season.

□ *Recuperation:* In order to progress toward peak strength levels, you must give your body the opportunity to recover adequately between strength workouts. Recuperation requires a very individual and delicate balance. Conventional wisdom suggests a minimum of 48 hours of rest between training sessions involving the same body part. Some muscles recover at different rates, however. For example, your quadriceps and lower back muscles may take up to 96 hours to recover, while your chest may require a minimum of 72 hours to be ready for more training. Smaller body parts, such as biceps and triceps, recover faster than do larger muscle groups (e.g., hips, upper back, shoulders, etc.). Also, the heavier and more intensely you train, the longer recovery time you will need. The programs designed in this book take into account the need for recuperation, and should give you a framework to work with as you become attuned to your body's need for recovery.

□ *Rest between sets:* How much you rest between sets is mostly related to how heavy you are lifting. During heavy training sessions, you should rest for three to four minutes before attempting a subsequent set. If you are working with light or medium weights, anywhere from one to one and a half minutes is sufficient. Mixing up your rest intervals is a great way to add variety to your training and can help lead to increases in overall strength.

□ *Lifting speed:* When it comes to the speed of individual repetitions, many contrasting opinions exist. Some experts feel lifting in a rapid fashion is more conducive to the needs of a basketball player. Others believe slower lifting allows a larger percentage of muscle fibers to come in to play, thus developing more strength. Personally, my beliefs tend to fall somewhere in the middle. Unless you are incorporating a high-intensity technique, such as forced repetitions or super-slow repetitions (you will read about these later), it is best to lift in a powerful, yet controlled manner without sacrificing proper exercise form. For example, when performing dumbbell presses, the concentric (upward) portion of the movement should last one second or so. The eccentric (lowering) phase of the lift should take approximately two seconds. Of course, there are a number of variables that will determine your lifting velocity such as amount of weight used, type of exercise, fatigue level, and the rest periods between sets.

❑   *Developing muscle balance:* It is important that basketball players and athletes in general have balanced muscle development. When antagonist muscle groups, such as quadriceps and hamstrings or chest and upper back, are out of balance (i.e., one body part is substantially stronger than the other), coordination and athletic performance can suffer. You also become more vulnerable to injury. Correctly performing the exercises documented later in the book, and adhering to the strength programs that are reviewed in chapter 8 will help ensure that your musculature will develop in a balanced, safe, and performance-enhancing manner.

❑   *Training the core:* Although balanced strength and muscle development is imperative for all athletes, as a basketball player, special attention must be given to training the core of your body. Your core or base, as it is frequently referred to, consists of the mid-section, hips, buttocks, lower back, and upper legs (quadriceps and hamstrings). This area of the body is involved in practically every movement a basketball player will make. Building strength in the core of your frame will greatly enhance your level of explosiveness and athleticism, which in turn will help you move faster, jump higher, and change directions quicker. All of these factors are obviously major ingredients for success on the basketball court.

❑   *Record keeping:* It is extremely important that you maintain accurate records concerning your strength training. At the very least, you should keep a training log that includes the date of workouts, the exercises used, the exercise order, the number of repetitions per set, the training poundage, the rest between sets, the total sets, and the workout time. Many advanced trainers also keep track of energy levels before and after workouts, recovery, diet and how it affects training, and the feel of each exercise. I have included a sample training log at the end of chapter 8.

❑   *Circuit training:* Circuit strength training consists of 10 to 15 exercise stations and entails moving from one exercise to another with little or no rest in between. The movements in the circuit typically work all parts of the body, usually from largest to smallest.

The technique experienced tremendous popularity in the late 1970s when Nautilus equipment and their inherent training methods came into vogue. Proponents of this system insisted that by completing one Nautilus circuit, wherein you perform every exercise to muscular failure, would allow you to not only reach peak strength levels, but also to substantially enhance your level of cardiovascular fitness as well. While these claims were not completely without merit, because circuit training does have its place in a strength training program, they have proven to be greatly exaggerated.

For a basketball player circuit training can provide variety, and can be especially useful when the athlete is pressed for time or when an individual is working out in a poorly equipped gym. Many athletes feel that moving through a particular circuit two or three times produces the best results. For the most part, however, the cardiovascular benefit derived from circuit training would be minimal for a basketball player, and should not take the place of a running program or on-court conditioning drills.

□ *Variety:* Never has the saying, "variety is the spice of life," been more appropriate as to when it relates to strength training. Mixing up your workout routine is essential to continued progress. A number of reasons can be advanced to support this factor.

First, changing your routine periodically keeps your muscles off balance, forcing them to adjust to the new demands placed upon them, thus producing strength gains. The body adapts fairly quickly, and must be constantly challenged with a variety of stimuli if improvement is to carry forward.

Second, mixing up exercises, set sequences, repetition schemes, and training intensities enables your workouts to be more interesting and creative. Nothing short circuits progress more than boredom. The tediousness of performing the same workout day after day and week after week can take its toll on even the most dedicated trainer.

Finally, being flexible with your training can also help you to avoid injury. Working muscles, tendons, and joints from the same angle with the same exercises for an extended number of sessions can eventually lead to injury.

□ *Limitations:* No matter how great your potential, at some point, you will hit your limit. It may seem odd to bring up limitations in a book dedicated to improvement, but being aware of your strengths and weaknesses (and yes, even your limits) is an important factor in getting the most out of your strength program. Having unrealistic expectations can be as damaging to progress as setting lackluster goals. You must realize that genetics, like it or not, play a big role in muscle and strength development. The key is to appreciate the improvement you make without becoming frustrated because you don't look like David Robinson after six months of strength training.

□ *Free weights versus machines:* The argument of free weights versus machines has been debated for years among bodybuilders, equipment manufacturers, and authors of weight-training books. The fact is that a place exists for both in a balanced strength training program. Free-weight exercises should, however, be the focal point of your routine. Machines are best utilized as a supplement to your free-weight work. A number of reasons support this recommendation, including:

• *Working the stabilizers:* The most compelling reason to build your routine around free weights, as opposed to machines, relates to stabilizing muscles and joints. Stabilizers help balance and control the weight during an exercise, while not being the primary area of the body involved in the movement. Working out with free weights stimulates these muscles and joints to a much greater degree than do machines. For instance, when comparing the back squat and machine leg press, it is easy to see why the squat is superior. While both movements develop the quadriceps, hamstrings, and gluteal muscles, the squat indirectly strengthens the lower back, shoulders, calves, ankles, wrists, and forearms. No machine ever invented has been able to duplicate this type of total-body stimulation.

• *Exercise variety:* An almost endless number of exercises exist that can be performed with free weights. The only limit is your imagination. And because every trainer's body is different, free-weight movements allow you the flexibility to most efficiently tailor your routine.

• *Range of motion:* Free weights allow your joints and limbs to move in their natural planes, thus providing a greater range of motion. Machines have a predetermined path of resistance, and the range of the exercise on a machine depends solely on the how the individual apparatus is constructed.

• *Satisfaction and confidence:* Confidence and satisfaction are two other variables that come from strength training with free weights. The feeling an individual gets from lifting a loaded barbell off the rack and successfully commanding his will against the resistance can be tremendous. You simply cannot replicate this feeling by strapping yourself into a machine and moving a bar back and forth on a predetermined track.

Of course, as was previously mentioned, machines should not be neglected altogether. Some exercise machines such as the leg extension, lat pulldown, leg curl, and triceps pressdown are basic to any balanced weight-training program. Machines can be particularly effective when you are rehabilitating from or working around an injury. The movements are generally more controlled and less taxing on the joints and tendons. Also, because changing poundage only entails moving a pin up or down a weight stack, as opposed to hauling big, cumbersome plates on and off a bar, machine workouts can be performed in less time than can free-weight sessions.

The point to remember is to use free weights as the basis of your routine and machines as a complement. By approaching your training in this manner, you will not be disappointed.

□ *Where to strength train:* You have many options when deciding where to train. Weight-training facilities range from large, glitzy health spas to your own basement or garage. In this section, various types of strength training facilities are reviewed, in which the advantages and disadvantages of each are discussed.

• *Commercial health clubs:* These clubs, or spas as they are sometimes called, cater to working men and women interested in becoming reasonably fit. Rarely, will you find a large number of serious athletes or hardcore weightlifters at facilities of this type. The atmosphere tends to be relatively social, with the emphasis on interaction among members. In fact, in the mid-1980s, with the fitness boom in full swing, health clubs were branded the singles bars of the future. Needless to say, this kind of environment can be very distracting to the serious training athlete.

Many commercial clubs do, however, have outstanding facilities. The weight equipment can be diverse and is generally well maintained (although some clubs tend to emphasize fancy machines rather than free weights). Many of these clubs also provide whirlpools, saunas, steam rooms, and massage treatment areas, along with aerobic and stretching classes.

Perhaps the biggest problems with commercial clubs, other than the all-too-frequent overly social atmosphere, are the large crowds, especially between 5:30 p.m. and 8:00 p.m., and the cost to join. Not only do some of these clubs charge hefty monthly membership fees, but initiation fees as well. So, if you don't mind crowds and the high cost doesn't bother you, these clubs may be for you.

• *Bodybuilding and power-lifting gyms:* Bodybuilding and power-lifting gyms were the precursors to the health spas. Nothing fancy about these facilities: most are dimly lit, somewhat dingy-looking places, with hundreds of pounds of free weights scattered about, and large, muscular men lifting huge amounts of iron. While somewhat intimidating at first, hardcore weightlifting gyms can be fantastic places to get great workouts. The atmosphere of clanging weights and intense trainers can help motivate you to outstanding efforts. I personally have lifted my heaviest weights in these surroundings. Another benefit of working out at hardcore gyms is the access you will have to many experienced lifters. Most of the members have strength trained seriously for many years, and are usually very willing to share their knowledge with you.

As with commercial clubs, bodybuilding and power-lifting gyms can get quite crowded at certain times of the day. Many are on the small side and can have limited space for stretching and warm-up. Most have shower facilities, but if you are looking for fancy steam rooms and saunas, these gyms are not for you. On the whole, however, these hardcore weightlifting gyms are recommended over heath clubs for basketball players and other serious athletes.

• *Team-training facilities:* If you have access to a well-equipped team-training facility, it is in your best interest to take advantage of it. Not only do these facilities usually have outstanding weightlifting apparatuses, but the camaraderie you develop with your teammates—as you all work toward the common goal of becoming stronger, better basketball players—can be invaluable.

Unfortunately, many team-training centers may only be available for use at certain times of the year, perhaps just during the school term. Also, even if the facility is accessible, it may be difficult to have your teammates in the same place year-round. Notwithstanding the problem with logistics, a team-training facility is arguably the best place to perform your strength workouts.

• *Home training:* Strength training at home can give you a tremendous amount of scheduling flexibility. Many athletes on tight schedules, with work and school commitments, find home training the most efficient way to get their workouts accomplished. Training sessions can be performed quickly with no waiting in line for equipment, and the travel time to the gym is only as long as it takes to walk to your garage or basement. In addition, if you prefer to work out at noon or midnight, the gym is always open (at midnight the other members of your household may not agree that the gym should be open, however).

Although home training has many advantages, there are some drawbacks. First, most home gyms are small and unable to accommodate the variety of equipment that a public gym can. This limitation can lead to less strength gains and boredom as well. Second, many trainers find it hard to motivate themselves without the collective energy of others working out around them. Third, unless you have a training partner on hand for all your home workouts, you will not have the benefit of a spotter for heavy lifts, a factor that can be both dangerous and strength restricting.

Whether home training is for you or not is a personal decision. All factors considered, home training should be used to supplement your gym workouts, unless of course you do not have access to a gym, or happen to have such outstanding home facilities that going to a public gym wouldn't be worthwhile. In any case, try to pick up some basic equipment for your home. An adjustable bench, barbell and weight set, a pair of adjustable dumbbells, and a chinning bar would be ideal. Having this equipment will come in handy, no matter where you decide to take the majority of your workouts.

☐ *What time of day to strength train:* This question may seem very simple, but as any basketball player involved in a strength-training program knows, when you train is almost as important as how you train.

Let's start with in-season weight workouts. During the season, your time is usually limited. When you consider the fact that lifting weights the day of and the day before a game is counterproductive, it may be hard to fathom when to strength train. In the competitive season, basketball should be your first priority, and although strength training continues to be extremely important, the game always comes first. Therefore, your weight workouts should be performed after practice, on off-days, and under the right circumstances, immediately following games. Practices, especially on the collegiate level, are so intense that you will need all your energy to compete for playing time. Strength training prior to a game will not allow you to be at your best.

Now, turn your attention to the off-season. As you know, this is the time of year to work on your basketball skills, improve weaknesses in your game, and to get your body strong and conditioned for the season ahead. The time of day you strength train is less important in the off-season. As such, it is recommended that you mix up your training times. Take some of your workouts before playing ball and some afterward.

In reality, however, with the preponderance of summer camps and off-season leagues around today, many young players will be tempted to cut back on their strength-training work in order to save their energy for these competitions. Unfortunately, college coaches and scouts, because of limited recruiting time, are forced to emphasize these summer showcases almost as much as regular season play when evaluating players. Regardless of what your summer schedule may be, you must discipline yourself to keep current with your strength-training program. In the long run, you will benefit much more by becoming a stronger and more explosive athlete than you would by scoring a few extra points in a summer-league game.

□ *When not to strength train:* There are some instances when you should not strength train. The most obvious being when you're injured, sick, overly tired, overtrained, or on a planned training break. It is also recommended that you stay out of the weight room the day of and the day before a game. Strength training this close to competition can be detrimental, since all your energy should be preserved for your performance efforts on the court.

□ *Overtraining:* Being in an overtrained state is the enemy of any athlete. It retards progress, inhibits performance, and can lead to injury. As a basketball player exercising with weights, you must remain acutely aware of how your body is responding to the stresses imposed by strength training. A delicate balance exists among workout frequency, training intensity, workout duration, and recuperation requirements.

There is good news and bad news when it comes to dealing with overtraining. First, the bad news. No one, at least to my knowledge, has ever achieved the perfect balance between training and rest. The good news, however, is that with experience and by following the principles detailed in this book, you will come close to training for optimal results. Your need for more or less exercise will become second nature to you, and overtraining will, for the most part, be avoided. The following points provide a list of the most common symptoms of overtraining, as well as some remedies if your body does become overtrained:

Symptoms
- ▶ Noticeable loss of strength and power
- ▶ Increased muscle, joint, and tendon soreness
- ▶ Lack of enthusiasm for workouts
- ▶ A preponderance of minor injuries
- ▶ Insomnia

Remedies
- ▶ Take a break from strength training (one to two weeks).
- ▶ Lower the weight you use and reduce the number of sets in your workout until you feel strong again.

- Mix up your routine (i.e., change exercises, set sequences, and training intensities).

- Include some extra stretching both before and after your strength workouts. This step will help reduce the level of lactic acid in your muscles, which causes soreness.

- If possible, analyze your training for the month prior to when you began to feel overtrained. This step will help you pinpoint possible problems and how to avoid them in the future.

☐ *Steroids:* Let me begin by saying, under no circumstances should a basketball player or any other athlete engage in the use of anabolic steroids or other so-called performance-enhancing drugs. On one hand, in today's competitive world of sports, the pressure to excel is tremendous. From junior high school on up to the professional ranks, athletes must constantly vie for medals, roster spots, and playing time. Unfortunately, this intense level of competition has led many athletes to experiment with performance enhancing drugs, such as steroids. The number of high-profile competitors who have been involved with steroids is too long to mention.

On the other hand, a number of serious side effects have been linked to steroid use. For example, the list of side effects includes liver cancer, various heart ailments, high blood pressure, raised cholesterol levels, and an impaired immune system function. Other side effects include premature baldness, insomnia, irritability, acne, impotence, and lower concentration levels.

Fortunately, very few (if any) basketball players have been involved in a serious steroid-related controversy. But, with the recent popularity of strength training among cagers, it certainly is possible that in the future, some players may be tempted to experiment. My staunch opinion is that a basketball player would benefit minimally from steroid use. Steroids tend to bulk the body to unnatural proportions. This added weight could have an adverse effect on a player's coordination and balance, as well as causing extra stress to his ligaments, tendons, and joints.

Most steroid users come from sports that traditionally rely on pure strength and size. Football players (mostly linemen), competitive weightlifters, bodybuilders, track and field athletes, wrestlers, and swimmers have long been suspected of using steroids and other performance-enhancing drugs. Most of these athletes cycle their use of the drug in order to peak for a particular event or match. For example, a weightlifter preparing for a competition would start with light doses of steroids three to four months before the event. Then, he would slowly increase his dosages until the date of the competition. After the event, his drug use would be discontinued. This approach would hardly work for a basketball player who must aspire to maintain peak performance levels for the better part of seven months.

Advanced Strength Training Methods

Splitting Your Routine

Bodybuilders have used variations of the split routine for years. It calls for dividing your body into two or three sections and training them in separate workouts. This method was developed to promote maximum intensity and adequate muscle recovery. Proponents of the split routine feel it is too taxing and time consuming to train the entire body in a single session. Also, muscle groups exercised later in a long workout tend to get short-changed due to lack of energy.

With regard to performing a split routine, it is recommended that a basketball player split his or her routine into two sections (refer to Table 6-1). Workout # 1 trains the pushing muscles of the upper body (chest, shoulders, and triceps) with the hamstrings and lower back. Workout # 2 trains the pulling muscles of the upper body (upper back, biceps, and forearms) with the hips and quadriceps. Abdominal muscles should be exercised four or five days per week. Calves and neck muscles will get adequate work without direct training.

In my experience, basketball players respond best to what is called an "every-other-day split," where you take at least one day off between strength-training sessions. In essence, you would weight train three days one week and four days the next week. This method allows for optimal recovery. Splitting your workouts also gives you the flexibility to strength train on consecutive days if your schedule allows. Since you are exercising antagonist muscle groups, no individual body part gets trained two days in a row. For example, workout # 1 would be performed on Mondays and Thursdays, workout # 2 would be done on Tuesdays and Fridays with Wednesdays and weekends off.

Workout # 1	Workout # 2
Chest	Upper Back
Shoulders	Biceps
Triceps	Forearms
Hamstrings	Hips
Lower Back	Quadriceps

Table 6-1. Recommended split-routine for basketball players

Emphasis Training

In order to achieve maximum results from your strength-training program, it is necessary to incorporate a method called emphasis training. This technique entails focusing on one major muscle group per workout with more intense training (i.e., heavier weights, extra sets, high intensity methods, etc.). Typically, smaller body parts, such as biceps and triceps, should not be emphasized in this type of training. In most instances, the muscle group being emphasized would be exercised at the beginning of a workout. This way you have the greatest amount of physical and mental energy at your disposal.

Weak-Point Training

Weak-point training is similar to emphasis training in that you prioritize an individual muscle group during a particular workout. As the term suggests, however, the body part you concentrate on will be one that responds slowly to training. For example, if your quadriceps and hips develop strength slowly and your upper back strengthens quickly, you would emphasize your legs in the majority of the training sessions in which you exercise these muscles together. Of course, this issue is an individual matter, and it is your responsibility to be aware of how your body responds to different training stimuli.

Heavy Days

Although some individuals may disagree, I believe that a place exists for heavy workout days in a basketball player's strength training program. During these sessions, heavy weights are lifted for low repetitions, using basic multi-joint exercises (e.g., bench presses, leg presses, upright rows, etc.). This type of training is most effectively used in the off-season and pre-season, but it can be selectively employed during the season as well.

Training with maximum weights not only builds tremendous muscle and tendon strength, it can also give you a great sense of satisfaction and confidence. There is nothing quite like the feeling of placing a loaded barbell back on the rack after an all-out set. Heavy workouts can also help you break through strength plateaus and sticking points in your training.

Some concerns relating to heavy training exist, however. The most prominent concern is the risk of injury. Tendons, joints, and ligaments are under enormous stress when handling heavy resistance. Therefore, it is necessary to warm up adequately before attempting heavy lifts. No less than three repetitions should be performed per set, and to ensure recovery, heavy lifting days should be accomplished no more than once a week for an individual body part. For safety reasons, an experienced spotter (or two if need be) must always be utilized.

Strength Training Twice a Day

This technique entails splitting an individual workout into two sections and performing the first part in the morning and the second part in the late afternoon or evening. Strength training twice in one day allows your metabolism to stay elevated for an extended period of time, which is ideal for athletes who want to lose excess weight. Many trainers report that their strength and energy levels are generally higher when performing two brief workouts, as opposed to a single longer one. Twice-a-day training should only be incorporated periodically during the off-season cycle, since the pre-season and in-season cycles have too many basketball-related responsibilities for such training to be feasible. Table 6-2 illustrates an example of how you might split your workout for twice-a-day training.

Workout #1:

Morning–Chest and shoulders   Evening–Triceps, lower back, and hamstrings

Workout #2:

Morning–Upper back, biceps, and forearms   Evening–Hips and quadriceps

---

Table 6-2. A sample twice-a-day training schedule

Explosive Lifting

For years, a raging debate has existed within the strength and conditioning community as to the usefulness of explosive weightlifting techniques that are used when performing exercises like the power clean and the snatch. While both camps have convincing arguments, along with ample studies to back them up, I personally feel that basketball players must be very careful in using explosive techniques. In fact, you can get terrific results from your strength training program without using explosive lifts. This is not to say this type of training is without merit, especially for athletes participating in sports such as football, but because of the special physical demands on basketball players, it is best to use caution. The following list outlines some of the reasons why basketball players should take care in using explosive techniques and lifts:

- *Complicated to learn.* Exercises such as the power clean and other explosive style lifts are extremely complex and time-consuming to learn. This time and energy, many feel, could be more constructively used by athletes to work on their basketball skills and their overall level of strength and conditioning. Furthermore, basketball players, because of their height and relatively long limbs, may have additional difficulty executing these lifts correctly.

- *Injury.* By far the biggest concern regarding explosive lifting techniques is the risk of injury. Ballistic movements put a great deal of stress on connective tissues and the musculature in general. Basketball players, because of the nature of their sport, are especially susceptible to the hazards of explosive lifting. The year-round aspect of the game and the tremendous pounding from sprinting, jumping, sliding, and cutting cause the body's physiological balance to be in a state of constant flux. Most injuries occur, whether on the court or in the weight room, when the body is not at full strength.

- *Momentum factor.* High velocity, explosive movements rely quite a bit on momentum, after the initial phase of the lift. Therefore, little resistance is placed on the muscles through the majority of the exercise. For this reason, some feel, explosive techniques are less effective for building strength than slower, more controlled methods of lifting.

If you choose to incorporate explosive lifts in your strength program, you should take the following precautions:

- Work closely with an experienced strength training specialist, an individual who has a background in Olympic weightlifting and body mechanics.

- If you have not done this type of lifting previously, spend a number of workouts focusing on technique with very little weight on the bar.

- Make sure you are thoroughly warmed up, not overly tired, and not suffering from any injuries.

- Wear a weightlifting belt during all explosive lifts.

If you ultimately decide to include these movements in your strength training program, they should only be employed in the off-season and pre-season. During the competitive season you will be energy-depleted much of the time, and while balanced strength training at a medium level of intensity will help maintain your strength and conditioning, overly taxing your body will lead to a decrease in performance and eventually to injury.

Specialized Techniques to Increase Intensity

You have a number of options for increasing the intensity level of your strength training workouts. The two most obvious are lifting heavier weights and shortening the rest intervals between sets. There are, however, other more complicated methods that can raise intensity to super-high levels. These techniques should only be incorporated into your routine after you've become thoroughly familiar with your strength level, comfortable with the exercise execution on all movements, and aware of your individual recovery requirements. Also, if used too frequently, high-intensity strength training will cause you to become overtrained in short order. A good rule of thumb is to only use a high-intensity technique on one body part per workout (some exceptions can be made such as when training shoulders and hamstrings together), and never work a muscle group more than once a week with high-intensity training. High-intensity cycles typically last four to six weeks.

The following examples illustrate some of the more popular and effective high-intensity techniques that are appropriate for basketball players. The list of examples also includes a few high-intensity methods that basketball players should stay away from.

• *Super sets.* Super sets are the king of high-intensity techniques. Super-setting entails performing two exercises, one after the other, with minimal rest between sets. Super-setting can be accomplished two ways. One method involves performing two exercises for different muscle groups (e.g., lateral raises for shoulders and chins for the upper back). The other option, referred to as "pre-exhaust" training, uses two movements for the same body part (e.g., machine flies and bench presses for the chest). While different body-part, super sets are an effective way to speed the pace of your workout and should be incorporated into your routine from time to time, "pre-exhaust" training is especially challenging and strength promoting. The basic premise behind this system of training is to fatigue the larger, stronger muscle first, so that the weak link in the strength chain (e.g., the triceps when performing an incline press), does not fail before the larger muscle you are attempting to train. In the incline press example, in order to work the upper chest muscles fully, you would execute a set of incline flies, followed immediately by a set of incline presses. The isolation movement (incline flies) will fatigue the upper chest to the extent where the triceps would actually be the stronger of the two muscles for a brief time, thus allowing the chest to be exercised to its capacity. Table 6-3 lists some of the best exercises to combine when employing super sets.

Super Sets – Different Muscle Group	Super Sets – Same Muscle Group
Incline Press/Pulley Row	Flat Fly/Bench Press
Push Press/Lat Pulldown	Incline Fly/Incline Press
Leg Extension/Leg Curl	Lateral Raise/Shoulder Press
Biceps Curl/Triceps Pressdown	Shrug/Upright Row
Pullover/Chin-Up	
Leg Curl/Straight Leg Dead Lift	

Table 6-3. Sample super-set combinations

• *Forced repetitions:* Forced repetitions are used to extend a set beyond the point of muscular failure. The key is to do as many repetitions in good form as you can without assistance. Then, when you can't lift the weight for another repetition, have your spotter give just enough help to allow you to reach the contracted position (e.g., arms extended in the bench press). Lower the weight under control and repeat with assistance the required number of repetitions (three to four repetitions after muscular failure are recommended).

- *Negative repetitions:* It has been estimated that your muscles are 30 percent stronger during the negative or eccentric (e.g., lowering the bar in the bench press) phase of an exercise. Negative training adheres to this premise to produce great strength gains.

You can incorporate negative training into your routine with either of two ways. One option is to complete a set to failure as you would with forced repetitions, but instead of having your spotter assist you gradually on the subsequent repetition, he would basically lift the weight for you, and then have you fight the resistance down to the starting point. Four to five negative repetitions are recommended.

The other alternative for performing negative repetitions is extremely intense. This technique, known in the bodybuilding community as "overload training," calls for loading the bar or weight stack with approximately 130 percent of your one-repetition maximum. Then, have your spotter, or spotters if need be, lift the weight to the fully contracted position (e.g., arms bent in the pulley row). Proceed by attempting to fight the resistance with all your strength until you reach the eccentric position (e.g., arms extended in the pulley row). This method of training can be considerably dangerous, and should only be performed when you're thoroughly warmed up and with experienced spotters on hand. Again, four to five negative repetitions works best for building strength.

- *Rest/pause training.* The rest/pause system of training involves working an exercise to muscular failure, pausing briefly (10 to 15 seconds), and then using the same weight, continuing the set for as many repetitions as possible. Two pauses per set are usually sufficient. This technique can be incorporated using any exercise, and is a fantastic way to build both strength and muscular endurance. It also enables you to shorten your workout substantially without sacrificing volume and intensity.

- *Super-slow training.* This method consists of taking eight to ten seconds to raise or pull a weight to the contracted position, as opposed to the typical one or two seconds. Many individuals feel lifting in this slow, deliberate manner forces the body to recruit more muscle fibers, thus building more strength and size. The amount of weight you use should be about 25 percent less than what you normally lift when exercising at a regular pace.

- *Stripping method.* Similar to some of the high-intensity techniques previously discussed, the stripping method involves completing a set to muscular failure. Then, instead of terminating the set, have your spotter remove some weight from the bar or weight stack, and immediately continue the set for as many repetitions as possible. The amount of weight removed depends on the particular exercise, your strength level, and how many times you plan on lowering the resistance. Three weight reductions per set are sufficient.

- *Partial repetitions and giant sets.* Two high-intensity methods you should stay away from as a basketball player are partial repetitions and giant sets. The former option entails working your muscles through a limited range of motion. Although this technique places additional stress on the working muscle, it also can decrease flexibility, and should be avoided unless you are training around an injury. The latter method is popular with many bodybuilders and fitness enthusiasts. It involves performing four different exercises consecutively without any rest between sets. This type of lifting obviously raises the exerciser's level of intensity, but in my opinion, puts too much stress on the body, especially for a basketball player who has many additional physical demands placed on him other than strength training.

Improving Your Basketball Skills with Strength Training

Strength Training and Shooting

One of the most common concerns basketball players have relating to strength training is that lifting weights will tighten their muscles and therefore hinder their shooting touch. When I was a young player many coaches and basketball people discouraged me from strength training for just that reason. Considering the majority of my points came on long-range jump shots, I was understandably wary. Fortunately, my father lifted weights, and he encouraged me to experiment. Needless to say this book would not have been written if I had not been pleasantly surprised.

Lifting weights in the correct manner through the full range of motion will not hamper your shooting. In fact, it will actually help to improve it. Through personal experience, and by training and observing hundreds of ballplayers, I am absolutely convinced of this. While strength training alone will not turn you into a great shooter (only three hundred practice shots a day can do that), it is possible to build additional strength that will enhance your shooting ability in a number of ways, including:

- First, because of increased strength in your hips, legs, shoulders, and arms, you will shoot more comfortably and accurately from longer distances. This factor will translate into more three-point baskets for perimeter players and increased shooting range for big men.

- Second, developing greater overall body strength will improve your ability to shoot and score, while absorbing contact. You will be able to maintain your balance even after a hard foul, and shots that previously would not have left your hand will now have the opportunity to go in the basket.

- Finally, added muscular endurance, developed through strength training, will enable you to shoot effectively from both the field and the free-throw line late in a game when fatigue sets in.

To ensure that your shooting touch is maintained, you should spend 10 to 15 minutes shooting the basketball immediately following your strength training sessions. Your shot and feel for the ball may be temporarily thrown off by your lifting efforts, but within a short time, as your muscles loosen, your shooting touch will return to normal. This approach is used in other sports as well. For example, Steve Young, former NFL star quarterback, tosses a weighted ball into a net, simulating a forward pass, after every upper-body strength workout.

Jump Higher with Strength Training

In no other sport besides basketball, with the possible exception of volleyball, does vertical jumping ability play such an integral part. Whether you are rebounding, attempting to block a shot, or shooting over a defender, you are leaving your feet in order to improve your position on the basketball court. It is no coincidence that some of the best and most exciting players in the NBA such as Kevin Garnett, Kobe Bryant, Steve Francis, and Vince Carter are all outstanding jumpers.

While there are other methods that can help improve jumping ability, such as plyometrics, which was designed to link strength with speed to produce power, weight training provides the base of strength that generates the force necessary to jump. Incorporating strength training, especially exercises like squats and lunges, into your overall conditioning program will help improve your vertical jump substantially. Also, recently much has been much written about how building additional lean muscle mass can help the body burn fat more efficiently. Having less fat will ensure you are not carrying excess weight, a factor that could inhibit your jumping ability.

Enhance Defensive Play through Strength Training

The game of basketball demands that players perform on both ends of the floor. No matter how prolific your offensive game, if you play poor defense, you will probably find yourself watching the action from the bench. Great teams at all levels build their success on the defensive end of the floor. In a sport of ups and downs, good and bad shooting games, poor calls by officials, and hostile crowds, defense can be the one constant. A player and a team can play good, solid defense every game regardless of circumstances.

Becoming a stronger and better-conditioned athlete will help you tremendously on defense. The following examples illustrate a few of the ways.

• *Post defense:* Players at all positions, from point guard to center, must have the ability to play good low-post defense. Strength training can help you become a better low-post defender. For example, building a strong, powerful base (hips, legs, lower back, and midsection) will enable you to keep your opponent from setting up where he wants to in the low post. Pushing an offensive player even a foot or two beyond the comfort zone down low can be the difference between two points and a defensive stop.

• *Fighting through picks and screens.* A good defensive player is able to fight over, around, and through picks and screens. This attribute takes great court awareness, desire, and strength. The stronger you are, especially in the upper body, the more effective you will be at carving out the space needed to stay with your man. Working through the labyrinth of screens sometimes resembles hand-to-hand combat. As a result, the more ammunition you have at your disposal (in this case, strength in your chest, shoulders, and triceps), the better you will fare at this demanding aspect of basketball.

• *Controlling penetration.* All efficient half-court offenses begin with the ballhandler moving the basketball toward scoring position. If the defense can disrupt this, even for a short time, the offensive set will most likely break down. Increasing strength in your lower body enables you to maintain your defensive stance for longer periods of time, thus making it easier to slide with your man and cut off his penetration. A defender with a powerful upper body can hinder an offensive player's progress by skillfully and forcefully using his hands, forearms, and shoulders. Knocking an opponent even slightly off balance on his way to the basket—without fouling of course—can be the key to a successful defensive stand.

• *Forcing turnovers.* Good defensive teams create turnovers. Many defensive-minded coaches not only keep track of forced turnovers, but deflections as well. Increasing your arm and hand strength through weight training enables you to knock balls out of opponents' hands more frequently. This additional strength also pays great dividends when double-teaming in the low post, trapping on the perimeter, and when fighting for a loose ball on the floor.

Improve Rebounding with Strength Training

By far the most physical aspect of basketball involves rebounding. Inside the paint, where big bodies battle for possession of the basketball at close proximity, strength and muscle are at a premium. The majority of the best board men in the NBA, from Tim Duncan to Ben Wallace, are also avid weight lifters. In order to become a good rebounder, you must develop a strong lower body. This attribute will enable you to obtain and maintain inside position, as well as enhancing your ability to jump quickly, powerfully, and explosively toward the basketball as it comes off the rim. To rebound effectively, your upper body also needs to be strong, especially in your hands, biceps, and upper back. Strength in these areas will enable you to pull rebounds off the glass and maintain possession of the ball in traffic.

Incorporating exercises such as step-ups, squats, and leg presses for the lower body and pulldowns, rows, and arm curls for the upper body will help ensure that you build the type of strength necessary to become a better rebounder. Of course, a number of attributes exist that help make a great rebounder—jumping ability, timing, and desire, just to name a few. But one thing is for sure; the stronger you are the better rebounder you will be.

Advance Your Offense through Strength Training

Along with improving your shooting, strength training consistently can also elevate many other facets of your offensive game, including the following:

• *Improving your first step.* Ask anyone familiar with the game of basketball what most outstanding offensive players have in common, and they will immediately tell you … a great first step. The initial step toward scoring position is the key to an effective offensive move. Regardless of how fast you happen to be, you can acquire this skill. Many productive scorers who do not possess great speed have tremendous first steps. One example that stands out is former Boston Celtic Larry Bird. Bird, a three-time NBA MVP, had the uncanny ability to drive by his defender using a simple pump fake, followed by a quick move right or left. What Bird lacked in speed, he more than made up for with his exceptional first step.

Developing and improving your first step involves three aspects. First, you must work on improving your quickness by incorporating on-court quickness drills into your conditioning program. Second, you must aspire to perfect your offensive moves and footwork until they become second nature. Finally, you must fully develop your level of strength through sound strength training. The additional strength you develop in your hips, legs, and body in general will make your movements quicker and more explosive, thus enhancing that all-important first step.

• *Low-post offense.* Several of basketball's premier offensive players score many of their points in the low post. All outstanding post scorers have the extraordinary ability to obtain and maintain position in the low blocks. This attribute requires tremendous strength in the hips, legs, lower back, and midsection. Working diligently in the weight room, especially on lower body exercises, will enable you to effectively position yourself down low. Some of the best post players in the game today, including Shaquille O'Neal, Tim Duncan, and Vlade Divac execute fundamental low-post techniques, such as pinning (sealing an opponent on your back prior to receiving the basketball) with great proficiency. Their tremendous strength allows them to position themselves close to the basket, ultimately leading to high-percentage shots. Of course, you must continue to work tirelessly on your low-post moves and shots, but strengthening your body to its full potential will enhance your offensive post game considerably.

• *Protecting your dribble.* With the emphasis on pressure defense in today's game, it is essential that backcourt players and ballhandlers in general have the ability to protect the basketball as they dribble up the court. Building upper-body strength, especially in the shoulders, chest, and triceps, enables you to use your non-dribbling arm as an effective obstacle for holding off defenders and preventing a steal or defection. Personally, I found in my own playing experience as a point guard that as I gained additional strength and muscle mass, my turnovers decreased significantly. The best exercises for increasing this type of strength are bench presses, shoulder presses, and lying triceps extensions. Developing extra power and explosiveness also enables you to split traps and double-teams aggressively, which leads to scoring opportunities for you and your teammates.

• *Improve your screening ability.* Anyone who has had the opportunity to watch basketball lately, especially professional basketball, has most likely noticed how the pick and role play has come back into vogue. Almost every team in the NBA uses some variation of the screen and role. Big, powerful players, such as Karl Malone of the Utah Jazz, have made a living setting solid screens on unsuspecting point guards, and then rolling to the hoop and receiving the basketball for easy shots. Screening off the ball is equally important to efficient offensive play, making it imperative that players at all positions perfect the art of setting picks at various areas and angles on the basketball floor. In fact, many teams rely on their guards and smaller players to screen for big men in order to force size mismatches. Karl Malone's teammate, John Stockton, at 6 feet and 175 pounds, is perhaps the best pick setter in the entire league.

To be an effective screener, you must have the ability to remain stationary and not give ground, while absorbing contact from the defensive player. This attribute takes great overall body strength. Boosting your strength level and increasing your muscle size in the weight room can help you considerably with this very physical aspect of the game. Although it won't show up on the stat sheet, and the fans may not acknowledge skillful screen setting, your coaches and teammates will surely appreciate your efforts.

• *Creating shooting space.* Regardless of how well you shoot the basketball, it will be of no use unless you can get your shot off consistently in game competition. Having the ability to create shooting space is extremely important for any basketball player, especially perimeter players who must be able to score off the dribble in one-on-one situations. Developing additional strength in the upper body enables you to use your shoulders to bump off defenders as you maneuver toward scoring position, thus creating adequate shooting room. This skill is exceptionally helpful when attempting to score from the mid-range area of the court (i.e., eight to sixteen feet from the basket). Coaches and scouts are always looking for players who have productive intermediate games. Many guards and small forwards have the ability to shoot accurately from three-point range, and can also take the ball to the basket and finish effectively, but very few combine these talents with a capable intermediate game. A big part of the reason is lack of upper body strength. Some of the NBA's best mid-range scorers such as Tracy McGrady, Allan Houston, Paul Pierce, and Ray Allen, are all strong and muscular through the shoulders, which enables them to create necessary shooting space. Among the exercises that can help you with this phase of your game are incline presses, push presses, upright rows, and lateral raises.

Performing at Your Best All Season Long

Not many people knowledgeable about the game of basketball would argue that the most important time of year to be at the top of your game is at the end of the regular season and during the post-season. Unfortunately, if you have participated in a full season of competitive basketball, complete with games, practices, travel, team meetings and film sessions, injuries, etc., you have no doubt experienced the uncomfortable feeling of your body wearing down as the campaign moves toward its latter stages. In order to counteract this deconditioning process and ensure that your peak performance levels are maintained, you must dedicate yourself to a well-planned, year-round strength training program. Working out with weights consistently and intelligently is the best way to build the type of strength and endurance that will guarantee you have something left in your tank late in the season. Just when other, less-dedicated players are beginning to fatigue, you will be hitting your stride. This attribute will translate into more points, more rebounds, and most importantly, more post-season wins.

Increasing Your Level of Confidence with Strength Training

Regardless of what sport you happen to participate in, having confidence in yourself and your ability is of paramount importance. Strength training is a superb way for basketball players to build their confidence levels. As your hard work in the weight room begins to show on the basketball court, you start to look forward to physical play, and instead of possibly being intimidated by bigger, stronger opponents, you welcome the challenge of matching strength and skill. Feeling stronger and becoming more muscular empower you, which ultimately leads to enhanced performance in-between the lines.

Prolonging Your Career with Strength Training

Training with weights can help you to prolong your basketball career. Many NBA players are competing effectively into their mid- to late thirties, and a few, such as John Stockton and Michael Jordan, are playing into their forties. Most of these players credit this set of circumstances to their improved level of conditioning—of which strength training is an integral part. If you are a professional player trying to continue your career, or a recreational basketball player looking to enjoy the game for as long as possible, strength training is an activity that can definitely help you in this regard.

CHAPTER 7

Strength Training Exercises

Chest Exercises

Bench Press

Muscles worked: Middle chest, anterior deltoids, and triceps

Exercise type: Multi-joint

Movement execution: Lying on your back on a flat exercise bench with your hands slightly wider than shoulder width, lift a loaded barbell off the rack and hold it with your arms extended above you. With your feet planted firmly on the ground and your buttocks against the bench, lower the weight under control to your mid-chest. Pause briefly, and proceed to press the bar back up to the locked out position.

Training tips and variations: It is important to keep your back as flat as possible to the bench during this movement (no arching). Arching your back, while enabling you to lift more weight, takes away from the intent of the exercise and could cause you to injure your lower back. In addition to using a barbell, the bench press can be performed with dumbbells or on various machines. Dumbbells tend to work the chest muscles through a greater range, and the emphasis of the resistance is on the outer pectorals.

 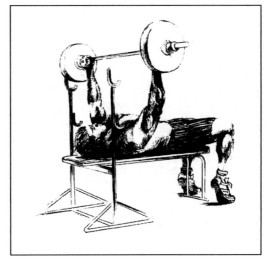

Incline Press

Muscles worked: Upper chest, anterior deltoids, and triceps

Exercise type: Multi-joint

Movement execution: Lying on an incline bench (at approximately a 45-degree incline), take a loaded barbell off the rack. Your grip should be slightly closer than that of the bench press (roughly shoulder-width). Lower the weight to the upper chest just below your neck. Pause briefly, and then press the resistance back to the starting position (arms locked).

Training tips and variations: The incline press puts a high degree of stress on the front deltoids. Therefore, in order to prevent injury, it is imperative that your shoulders are sufficiently warmed up before attempting to lift heavy weight in this movement. As with the bench press, the incline press can be executed with dumbbells or machines. In addition to increasing the range of motion, working with dumbbells allows you to easily vary the angle of the incline bench from almost flat to almost upright. The higher the angle of the bench, the more you work the upper chest. With a flatter bench, the stress shifts to the lower portion of the chest.

Flat Bench Fly

Muscles worked: middle chest

Exercise type: single-joint

Movement execution: Lie on a flat exercise bench with two moderately heavy dumbbells held at arms' length above you. With your palms facing each other, lower the weights with bent arms to just below the level of your body. After pausing at the bottom for a count, bring the dumbbells back up to the straight-arm position as if you were hugging someone.

Training tips and variations: Correct form must be maintained when performing flyes, since a relatively strong tendency exists to turn the movement into a press, especially toward the latter portion of a set when your muscles are fatigued. To discourage this from occurring, keep the level of resistance you use with this exercise reasonably light. Flyes can be executed very effectively using a variety of exercise machines. In fact, many trainers actually prefer machine flyes to dumbbell flyes. Using these machines helps to isolate the pectoral muscles throughout the entire range of the movement, as well as allowing for an intense isometric contraction when the arms are brought together.

 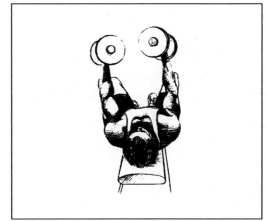

Dip

Muscles worked: Lower chest, anterior deltoids, and triceps

Exercise type: Multi-joint

Movement execution: Start by balancing at arms length above dipping or parallel bars. Lower yourself under control until your shoulders are slightly above the bars. Then push upward to the arms' extended position.

Training tips and variations: When performing dips, the farther you lean forward, the more stress you will put on the lower chest. As you move upright, the stress becomes greater on the triceps. Some dipping bars allow you to vary your hand placement. The wider the grip, the more you exercise the outer chest. Dipping on the narrow area of the bars puts more stress on the inner chest and triceps. Extra resistance can be added by using a weight harness or by having your training partner place a dumbbell between your crossed ankles. For those individuals who are unable to perform more than six repetitions, most gyms have a machine called a Gravitron, which allows you to perform dips with a percentage of your body weight.

 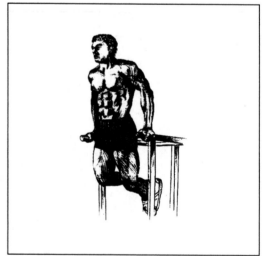

Incline Fly

Muscles worked: Upper chest

Exercise type: Single-joint

Movement execution: Lying on an incline bench (at an approximately 45-degree angle), hold two moderately weighted dumbbells overhead with your palms facing each other. Lower the dumbbells slowly, bending your elbows slightly, to just under the height of the bench. Bring the weights back to the starting point in the same motion as you would with flat-bench flyes (hugging motion).

Training tips and variations: As with flat-bench flyes, the dumbbells should be relatively light, as not to turn the movement into a press. Incline flyes are very effective in a super-set with barbell incline presses. There are machines that duplicate this movement, but most are awkward to use and should be avoided.

Cable Crossover

Muscles worked: Middle chest

Exercise type: Single-joint

Movement execution: Stand with your knees partially bent, and while leaning slightly forward at the waist, grab hold of the handles attached by cables to overhead pulleys. Bring your hands together in unison in a hugging motion until they touch. Pause, and then return under control to the starting position.

Training tips and variations: This exercise is used mostly by experienced bodybuilders and may take awhile to get used to. Be patient and try to find the right groove for your body. If you choose to incorporate cable crossovers into your routine, be sure and perform them at the end of your chest workout, because they are most effective for strength building when the chest muscles are fatigued.

Decline Press

Muscles worked: Lower chest, anterior deltoids, and triceps

Exercise type: Multi-joint

Movement execution: Lying on a decline bench, place your hands on the bar, slightly wider than your shoulders. Proceed to lift the weight off the rack, and lower it under control to the lower portion of the chest. Pause briefly, and then push the resistance straight up to the arms-extended position.

Training tips and variations: Because dips essentially exercise the same muscle groups as decline presses, you would not want to do these two movements in the same workout. As with bench presses and incline presses, you can use dumbbells and various exercise machines to perform declines.

Back Exercises

Chin-Up

Muscles worked: Upper latissimus dorsi, biceps, and forearms

Exercise type: Multi-joint

Movement execution: Grab hold of a chinning bar with an overhand grip. Your hands should be spaced several inches wider than shoulder-width apart. Pull yourself up so that the bar touches your upper chest. Lower yourself under control to the arms-extended position.

Training tips and variations: When performing conventional chin-ups, arching your back slightly during the concentric portion (pulling up) of the movement is suggested. This action will ensure that you stress the upper back fully. Otherwise, your biceps and forearms will receive the majority of the stimulation. Perhaps no other exercise has as many variations as the chin-up. Chins can be executed while touching the bar behind the neck, with an underhand grip, with almost countless hand spacings, using a double handle bar, and with grip-enhancing straps. As with dips, a Gravitron can be used to enable you to off-load part of your body weight mechanically. Furthermore, weight can be added either with a harness or by placing a dumbbell between your crossed ankles.

Seated-Cable Row

Muscles worked: Lower latissimus dorsi, posterior deltoids, biceps, and forearms

Exercise type: Multi-joint

Movement execution: Seated in a cable-row apparatus, grip the handle firmly and have your feet supported in front of you. With your knees partially bent, proceed to lower the resistance to the arms-extended position (i.e., the starting point). Then, pull the weight back toward your body, arching your back slightly, and finally touching the handle to your abdomen. Continue by slowly returning the resistance to the starting position.

Training tips and variations: The negative phase of this exercise should be performed in a very controlled fashion. It is important to fully stretch your back at the bottom of the movement before attempting another repetition. Because the pulley machine allows for great control during both the eccentric and concentric portions of the exercise, seated-cable rows are excellent for incorporating such high-intensity techniques as super-slow repetitions and negative repetitions. One exercise that is commonly used in place of or in addition to seated-cable rows is the bent-over-barbell row. Although this exercise can build tremendous power in the middle back, the movement puts too much strain on the lower back. As such, the risks far outweigh the benefits in this case.

One Arm Dumbbell Row

Muscles worked: Middle and lower latissimus dorsi, biceps, and forearms

Exercise type: Multi-joint

Movement execution: Place one hand and one knee on a flat exercise bench. Grab a sufficiently heavy dumbbell from the floor and, keeping your back flat, lift the weight up to your side. Squeeze at the top, and proceed to lower the resistance under control to the extended arm position.

Training tips and variations: Of all the back exercises, the one-arm dumbbell row gives you the best opportunity to really test your strength. Because your lower back is totally supported, it is possible to use very heavy weights without fear of injury. This movement can be executed with a cable, using a floor-level pulley. There are also a few new machines that allow you to do single-arm rows. Dumbbells, however, are by far the most effective way to perform this exercise and should be used whenever possible.

Pulldown

Muscles worked: Upper latissimus dorsi, biceps, and forearms

Exercise type: Multi-joint

Movement execution: Using a lat machine, grab the bar with a fairly wide, overhand grip. Then, arching your back slightly, pull the bar down until it touches the top of your chest. Pause, and proceed to extend your arms back to the starting point.

Training tips and variations: Pulldowns are extremely effective when used in a super set with some type of pullover movement. Similar to chin-ups, this exercise allows you to vary your hand placement and execution in many ways. For example, you can pull the bar down behind your neck, use an underhand grip, or change your grip spacing from very wide to exceptionally narrow. Unlike chins, because you can exercise with less than your own body weight, you can perform additional repetitions.

 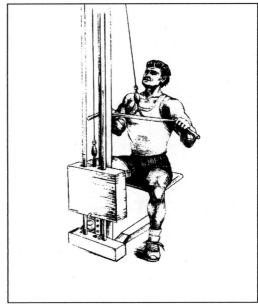

T-Bar Row

Muscles worked: Middle latissimus dorsi, biceps, and forearms

Exercise type: Multi-joint

Movement execution: Standing with your knees flexed, bend at the waist and grab hold of the handles of a T-Bar. Pull the resistance toward your stomach in a smooth, powerful manner. Pause briefly at the contracted position, and keeping your back stationary, lower the weight under control to the arms-extended position.

Training tips and variations: T-Bar rowing, while an effective way to train the back, puts a good deal of strain on your lower back. Therefore, it is imperative that you keep your knees sufficiently bent in order to distribute the stress evenly throughout your lower body. Wearing a weightlifting belt is strongly recommended when performing T-Bar rows. A number of exercise machines exist that simulate this movement, many of which allow you to lie prone, with your weight supported by a bench pad, thereby reducing the level of stress on your low-back region.

Pullover

Muscles worked: Latissimus dorsi

Exercise type: Single-joint

Movement execution: Lie on your back on a flat exercise bench. Take hold of a barbell with a shoulder-width, overhand grip and let it hang down toward the floor by bending your elbows. Keeping your arms stationary, pull the resistance up so that the bar comes to rest on the middle of your chest.

Training tips and variations: Unlike most exercises in a basketball player's strength program, the pullover is best performed on a machine. Pullover machines are one of the most valuable pieces of equipment in any gym. They provide resistance throughout the entire range of motion, and can be used effectively for extended sets and super sets. Athletes with shoulder or neck problems should use caution when executing pullovers.

 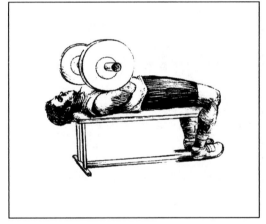

Hyperextension

Muscles worked: Erector spine (low back)

Exercise type: Single-joint

Movement execution: Position yourself so you are facedown across a hyperextension bench, with your feet underneath the footpads. With your arms folded across your chest, bend straight down over the pad. Then, come back up under control until your torso is approximately parallel to the floor.

Training tips and variations: Resistance can be added to hyperextensions by holding a barbell plate to your chest. This movement can be executed effectively by using a specially designed back machine or by performing the exercise on the floor without weighted resistance.

 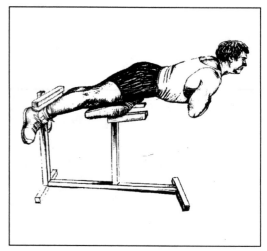

Shoulder Exercises

Shoulder Press

Muscles worked: Anterior deltoids, medial deltoids, and triceps

Exercise type: Multi-joint

Movement execution: Seated on a flat exercise bench, grab a loaded barbell off the rack with a slightly wider than shoulder-width grip, and lower it down behind your neck (starting position). Press the weight straight up to the arms-extended position, and then lower it slowly back to the starting position.

Training tips and variations: It is extremely important to thoroughly warm up your entire shoulder girdle before attempting heavy shoulder presses. This movement creates a good deal of tension throughout the shoulder region, and if the muscles are not prepared properly, an injury can occur. The shoulder press has many possible variations. For example, it can be executed with dumbbells, various machines, standing, or by lowering the bar to the front of your neck. All are efficient, and mixing up the way you perform this exercise is strongly encouraged.

Push Press

Muscles worked: Anterior deltoids, upper chest, upper quadriceps, and triceps

Exercise type: Multi-joint

Movement execution: In a standing position, grab a barbell off a power rack with a shoulder-width grip and rest it on your upper chest just below your neck. Start by bending your knees slightly, and then simultaneously straighten your legs and push the weight straight up overhead to the arms-extended position. Lower the barbell under control back to the starting position.

Training tips and variations: During the positive (lifting) phase of the push press, make sure to keep your body positioned under the weight throughout the movement. Not doing so could cause a loss of balance and possible injury. Many trainers substitute a Smith machine for a barbell when performing push presses. Dumbbells can also be used but tend to be awkward, especially when lowering the resistance. Using a barbell is the most effective way for performing the push press and should be used the majority of the time for this exercise.

Lateral Raise

Muscles worked: Medial deltoids

Exercise type: Single-joint

Movement execution: Standing with your knees slightly bent, take two moderately weighted dumbbells and bring them to your sides at arms length. Raise the weights away from your sides, as if you were pouring a pitcher of water, until your arms are just above parallel to the floor. Lower the dumbbells slowly, resisting the weight on the way down.

Training tips and variations: For best results, lateral raises should be performed with moderate-to-light weights. To involve more of the rear deltoids, turn your wrists slightly at the top so the back of the dumbbell is higher than the front. This movement can be executed while seated or on a variety of exercise machines, and is very effective when incorporated in a super set with shoulder presses.

Upright Row

Muscles worked: Trapezius, medial deltoids, posterior deltoids, biceps, and forearms

Exercise type: Multi-joint

Movement execution: In a standing position, grasp a loaded barbell with an overhand grip and with your hands five-to-eight inches apart. Starting with your arms extended, lift the resistance straight up, with the bar as close to your body as possible, to a point just below your chin. Pause briefly at the top, and then lower the barbell under control back to the starting position.

Training tips and variations: To involve more of the deltoids when performing upright rows, widen your grip. To hit the trapezius muscles harder, narrow your grip. This movement can be executed with a floor pulley, as well as with dumbbells, but using a barbell is the most effective option.

Bent Lateral Raise

Muscles worked: Posterior deltoids

Exercise type: Single-joint

Movement execution: Seated near the end of a flat exercise bench, lean over at the waist and grab two fairly light dumbbells from the floor. Keeping your body balanced, lift the weights out to either side, turning your wrists so your thumbs are pointed downward. Your arms will be slightly bent during execution, and the weights should be lifted just above the height of your head before returning to the starting position.

Training tips and variations: For best results, bent laterals should be performed with light weights. The key is to execute the movement in a strict fashion and try to focus on exercising the rear deltoids fully. In addition to being seated, bent lateral raises can be done standing, lying prone on an incline bench, or using a variety of machines.

Shoulder Shrug

Muscles worked: Trapezius

Exercise type: Single-joint

Movement execution: Grasp a loaded barbell off a waist-high rack with an overhand, shoulder-width grip. Step away from the weight rack, holding the barbell with your arms extended. Keeping your arms extended, shrug your shoulders (i.e., attempt to touch your shoulders to your ears). Pause at the top, and then lower your shoulders slowly back to the starting point.

Training tips and variations: Because of the heavy weight needed to stimulate the trapezius muscles, it is important that you bend your knees sufficiently when performing standing barbell shrugs. This action takes pressure off your lower back. Wearing a weightlifting belt is also advised. Shrugs can be executed with dumbbells (either seated or standing), Universal gym equipment, or on specially designed shrugging machines.

Leg/Hip Exercises

Squat

Muscles worked: Hips, quadriceps, buttocks, hamstrings, and lower back

Exercise type: Multi-joint

Movement execution: Standing, with your feet approximately shoulder-width apart, rest a loaded barbell across your shoulders. With your hands balancing the bar, bend your knees and lower yourself until your thighs are just below parallel to the floor. Keeping your head up and your back straight, drive yourself back up to the standing position.

Training tips and variations: Many trainers prefer that their heels are elevated on a low block of wood (e.g., a 2" x 4") for balance when squatting. Also, if you have never squatted before, it is advisable to keep the weight light until you feel thoroughly comfortable with the movement. There are a number of machines, such as the Smith Machine, that allow you to perform squats. While not as effective as the barbell version, machine squats provide a nice change of pace and tend to isolate the quadriceps to a greater degree. To work different areas of your thighs, you can change your foot position while exercising. A slightly wider stance with your toes pointed out hits the inside of the thighs, while a slightly narrower stance with your toes pointed in, exercises the outside of the quadriceps.

Lunge

Muscles worked: Quadriceps, buttocks, hips, calves, and hamstrings

Exercise type: Multi-joint

Movement execution: Standing upright holding a barbell across your back, step forward, bend at the knees, and bring your back knee close to the floor. Then, proceed by driving yourself under control back to the standing position.

Training tips and variations: Lunges can be performed by alternating legs every repetition or by doing separate sets for each leg. Separate-leg sets tend to work the leg muscles more intensely. As with squats, before attempting to use heavy weights, become familiar with proper technique. Lunges can be performed with dumbbells held at your sides or on a Smith machine. It is also possible to lunge at different angles for variety. Lunges are not advisable if you have knee problems.

Leg Press

Muscles worked: Quadriceps, hips, buttocks, and hamstrings

Exercise type: Multi-joint

Movement execution: Seated in a leg-press machine, place your feet on the top of the leg press, with your toes pointed slightly outward, approximately shoulder-width apart. Unlock the weight and bend your knees, lowering the resistance as far as possible. Press the weight back up through your heels to just short of the legs-extended position.

Training tips and variations: As mentioned above, it is suggested that you do not lock your knees at the top of the leg press. This step allows you to maintain tension on your thighs throughout the movement (something you can't accomplish with squats), and prevents the possibility of injury to the knee joint. Many trainers feel they can use more weight in this exercise than in the squat, because there is very little pressure on the lower back. A variety of leg-press machines are available. The same principles apply, regardless of what equipment you have. As with squats, you can alter your foot position to work different areas of your thighs.

Straight-Legged Dead Lift

Muscles worked: Hamstrings and lower back

Exercise type: Multi-joint

Movement execution: Standing, take hold of a barbell with an overhand, shoulder-width grip. Keeping your legs straight, bend at the waist with your back straight and your arms extended. Pause momentarily when your torso is parallel to the floor, and then straighten slowly back to the standing position.

Training tips and variations: It is best to perform straight-legged dead lifts in a deliberate manner, especially when incorporating heavy weights. Although many trainers do this exercise with both of their feet flat on the floor, it is more effective to stand on a specially designed box (approximately one and a half feet high). This way of doing the exercise allows for maximum stretch and enables you to exercise the hamstrings fully.

Leg Extension

Muscles worked: Quadriceps

Exercise type: Single-joint

Movement execution: Using a leg-extension machine, sit and anchor your feet under the cushions. Then, extend your lower legs up as high as possible and hold for a count. Lower the weight under control to the starting point.

Training tips and variations: Leg extensions can be executed one leg at a time for variety, and are great for incorporating super-slow repetitions.

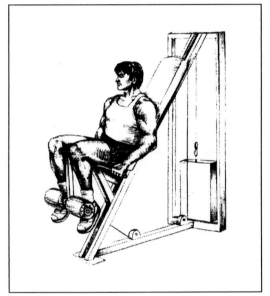 

Leg Curl

Muscles worked: Hamstrings

Exercise type: Single-joint

Movement execution: Lying on your stomach on a leg-curl machine, place your heels under the pads. Proceed by pulling your heels up as close as possible to your buttocks, while keeping your body flat on the machine. Pause at the top, and lower the resistance back to the starting position.

Training tips and variations: As with leg extensions, you can train one leg at a time when performing leg curls. Super-slow repetitions and negative repetitions are also easy to execute on a leg-curl machine. In addition to conventional leg curls, some gyms have equipment that allows you to isolate one leg at a time from a standing position.

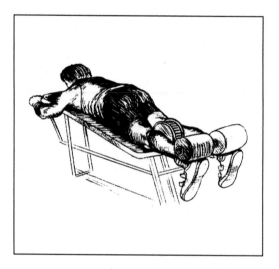 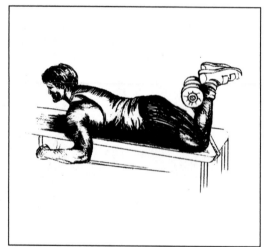

Step-Up

Muscles worked: Hips, quadriceps, buttocks, and calves

Exercise type: Multi-joint

Movement execution: With a barbell resting across your shoulders and your hands balancing the resistance, step up on to a box (the height of the box can vary depending on your stature, strength level, and objectives), as if you were climbing stairs. Pause at the top with your legs straight, and then step down carefully back to the standing position.

Training tips and variations: Step-ups can be performed either by alternating legs every repetition or by doing one complete set with your left leg, followed by one complete set with your right leg. For variety, dumbbells held at your sides can be used.

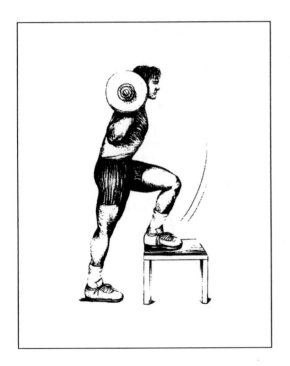 

Biceps Exercises

Barbell Curl

Muscles worked: Biceps

Exercise type: Single-joint

Movement execution: Standing with your knees slightly bent, grasp a loaded barbell off a waist-high rack with an underhand grip of approximately shoulder width. Let the bar hang down with your arms straight, and then curl the weight up smoothly to your upper chest, keeping your back straight and your elbows close to your torso. Pause at the top, and then proceed to lower in a controlled fashion back to the starting position.

Training tips and variations: In order to add intensity to barbell curls and squeeze out a few extra repetitions, a small amount of body swing is acceptable. A floor pulley or dumbbells can be used from time to time for variety, but the barbell version is by far the best for building strength and size in the biceps.

Incline Curl

Muscles worked: Upper biceps

Exercise type: Single-joint

Movement execution: Seated on an incline bench, hold a dumbbell in each hand with your arms fully extended and your palms facing each other. With your elbows in, curl both dumbbells in unison, while slowly twisting your palms upward, to your front deltoids. Then, lower the weights slowly back to the starting point (palms facing each other).

Training tips and variations: It is important that you pause at the bottom of the movement to prevent yourself from using momentum for the next repetition. The dumbbells can be lifted one at a time for variety.

Hammer Curl

Muscles worked: Forearms and biceps

Exercise type: Single-joint

Movement execution: Seated at the end of a flat exercise bench, grasp a dumbbell in each hand. With your arms fully extended at your sides and your palms facing each other, curl the weights straight up to your front deltoids, keeping your wrists stationary throughout. Pause at the top, and then lower the dumbbells under control back to the starting position.

Training tips and variations: Hammer curls can also be performed while standing. As with incline curls, you must pause at the bottom of the movement to prevent momentum from affecting the following repetition.

Preacher Curl

Muscles worked: Lower biceps

Exercise type: Single-joint

Movement execution: Seated on a preacher bench with your chest against the pad, grasp a barbell with an underhand grip from the rack. Without rocking backward, curl the bar up to approximately forehead height. Pause at the top, and then lower the barbell slowly back to the arms-extended position.

Training tips and variations: When performing preacher curls, many individuals feel it is helpful for strength development to squeeze the biceps muscle intensely at the top of the movement before lowering. For variety, an E-Z curl bar can be used in place of a straight bar. Dumbbells can also be utilized.

Triceps Exercises

Lying Triceps Extension

Muscles worked: Triceps

Exercise type: Single-joint

Movement execution: Lying on a flat exercise bench with your head just off the edge, take hold of a barbell with a slightly closer than shoulder-width apart grip and place it just above your forehead. Keeping your elbows stationary, push the resistance up by extending your arms to the locked-out position. Then, lower the weight slowly back to the starting position.

Training tips and variations: Many trainers feel that using an E-Z curl bar when performing lying triceps extensions gives more control and a slightly increased range of motion. If you do not have access to a bench, it is possible to do this exercise on the floor.

Triceps Press-Down

Muscles worked: Triceps

Exercise type: Single-joint

Movement execution: Grasp a short bar from an overhead pulley with an overhand grip and your hands six to eight inches apart. With your elbows close to your torso and your knees slightly bent, push the bar down, locking your arms at the bottom. Release, and then bring the resistance back to the starting point (approximately chin height) before repeating.

Training tips and variations: For variety, you can use a different shaped bar, a specially designed rope, or a lat machine. Also, you can experiment with your grip placement, or even use an underhand grip for added stretch.

Seated Triceps Extension

Muscles worked: Triceps

Exercise type: Single-joint

Movement execution: Sit on the end of a flat exercise bench and grasp a barbell overhand with your hands ten to twelve inches apart. Bring the weight behind your head until your upper arms are parallel to the floor (the starting position). Then, extend your arms, pushing the bar overhead to the locked-out position.

Training tips and variations: Some trainers prefer to perform this movement standing, as opposed to sitting. Dumbbells, an E-Z curl bar, or an extension machine can be used for variety.

 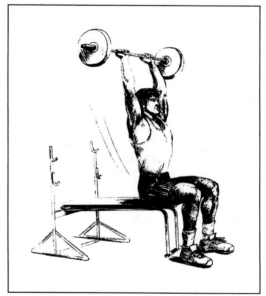

Close-Grip Bench Press

Muscles worked: Triceps, inner chest, and front deltoids

Exercise type: Multi-joint

Movement execution: Lie on a flat exercise bench and grab a loaded barbell off the rack with your hands three to four inches apart. As you would with the conventional bench press, lower the weight down to the middle portion of your chest and then proceed to press it back up to the arms-extended position.

Training tips and variations: You will not be able to handle nearly as much weight as you would in the regular bench press. Your concentration should be on isolating the triceps muscle as much as possible. In addition to a barbell, close-grip bench presses can be executed effectively on a Smith machine.

Abdominal Exercises

Legs-in-the-Air Sit-ups

Muscles worked: Lower abdominal region

Exercise type: Single-joint

Movement execution: Lying on your back with your hands clasped behind your head and your legs in the air as high as possible, crunch up, bringing your head to your knees. Hold momentarily at the top and then proceed to lower yourself back to the starting position.

Training tips and variations: Although your concentration should be on working your lower abdominal area, you can, by bending your knees, exercise your upper midsection more directly. For variety, you can keep your hands at your sides or have them pointing straight up toward the ceiling when crunching. Additional resistance can be incorporated into the exercise by holding a medicine ball or a barbell plate behind your head.

Bench Crunch

Muscles worked: Upper abdominal region

Exercise type: Single-joint

Movement execution: Lying on your back on the floor with your hands clasped behind your head, place your feet and lower legs over a flat exercise bench. Then sit up, raising your head toward your knees. Pause at the top, and lower your body under control back to the floor.

Training tips and variations: To involve more of your lower midsection, lift your pelvis off the floor during the up phase of the movement. To add resistance to bench crunches, you can hold a barbell plate or a medicine ball behind your head. A number of exercise machines exist that also simulate the crunching motion.

Side Sit-up

Muscles worked: Oblique

Exercise type: Single-joint

Movement execution: Lie on your side and raise your outside leg upward. Then, with your upper hand on the side of your head and your lower arm braced on the floor, crunch sideways toward the raised leg, feeling the oblique contract as you move upward. Hold briefly at the top, and then return your torso to the floor, leaving your outside leg raised throughout.

Training tips and variations: Side sit-ups are most effective when a high number of repetitions are performed.

Twisting Sit-up

Muscles worked: Oblique, serratus, and upper abdominal region

Exercise type: Multi-joint

Movement execution: Lie on your back on the floor with your knees bent and your feet flat on the floor. Then, cross your left leg over your right knee and clasp your hands behind your head. Proceed by twisting up with your torso, ending by pointing your right elbow to your left knee. Then, lower your body back to the floor. Then, do the same for the opposite side.

Training tips and variations: It is best to perform twisting sit-ups at the end of your abdominal workout.

Hanging Leg Raise

Muscles worked: Lower abdominal region

Exercise type: Single-joint

Movement execution: Start by hanging at arm's length from a chinning bar with an overhand grip and your hands shoulder-width apart. Then, lift your legs straight in front of you, while keeping your upper body relatively straight. Hold for a count, and finish by lowering your legs back down to the starting position without letting your feet touch the floor.

Training tips and variations: Many trainers use straps in order to enhance their grip when performing hanging leg raises. When you cannot execute another repetition with your legs straight, it is possible to extend the set by bending your knees. A variation of this movement can be performed on a vertical bench, where you support yourself by the elbows, thus taking the grip element out of the exercise.

CHAPTER 8

Year-round Strength Training Program for Basketball

Designing a personalized strength training program for basketball players can be extremely challenging. Tremendous demands come with participating in competitive basketball, and finding the time, energy, and motivation to build and maintain strength takes considerable planning and effort.

The overall objective of a basketball player's strength training program is relatively simple to explain, but not easy to achieve. An athlete must aspire to reach peak strength levels on the first day of organized practice, and maintain that strength throughout the competitive season. In order to accomplish these lofty goals, the athlete needs to adhere to three basic concepts, which are referred to as the three C's for strength training success—consistency, creativity, and concentration.

Consistency

If you hope to be successful with your strength training program, you must be consistent. This factor involves getting to the gym regularly and training hard when you are there. Lifting weights is the ultimate cumulative activity. The weight you lift one week builds on the weight you lifted the previous week. When it comes to building strength, there are no shortcuts and no exceptions.

Creativity

While it is certainly necessary to follow an organized strength training program, in order to progress optimally, you must be *creative* within your routine. Oftentimes, individual creativity is discouraged, as the majority of strength coaches have their athletes follow very rigid workout programs. It should be understood, however, that strength training is as much an art as it is a science, and that every individual has unique characteristics when it comes to developing strength and muscle. For example, most larger-framed athletes respond to fast-paced training with medium weights (for them) and somewhat higher repetitions. For these individuals, gaining strength and muscle comes easy. Their major concern is staying lean and muscularly toned. On the other hand, athletes who are naturally slim and small boned achieve the best results from using heavy loads (for them) with low repetitions and ample rest periods between sets. Building size and strength is the priority for an individual with this body type, and gaining too much weight is never a concern.

Another area where creativity is required is when scheduling workouts. Minor injuries, low energy levels, and time constraints can wreak havoc on even the best planned program. Being flexible and creative with your training is the foremost defense against these unexpected, but inevitable, occurrences. With experience, you will eventually develop an intuitive feel for when to push ahead with heavy, intense training, and when to lighten the resistance or skip a planned workout altogether. Once accustomed to the basics of strength training, by all means experiment creatively and discover what works best for you.

Concentration

Concentration is an often-overlooked aspect of strength training. It is, however, of paramount importance. You must try diligently to bring full *concentration* to every exercise, set, and repetition during your workout. Unfortunately, this is easier said than done, given the fact that your mind can go off in a million different directions. Unlike participating in a game or practice, where concentration comes about naturally due to outside stimuli, training with weights is a personal undertaking that demands constant, mindful attention. The goal is to feel your muscles working throughout the entire movement, and to discipline yourself to work as hard as possible. Remember, only you know if maximal effort is being given.

Two common obstacles to concentration exist during a strength training session. One involves thinking about your next set while performing your current set. The other is the tendency to lose focus late in the workout as the body tires. Avoiding these pitfalls takes awareness and discipline—awareness of when the mind begins to wander, and the discipline to bring your attention back to the current set. The faster you can return mentally to the task at hand, the more effective your training will be.

Lifting weights with full concentration also has the added benefit of allowing you to detect minor discomforts that may be precursors to injury. I know from personal experience that the majority of strength training injuries develop over a number of workouts. If you can notice the early warning signs and act accordingly (i.e., change exercises, lighten the resistance, discontinue your workout, etc.), many of the injuries that you might otherwise incur can be avoided.

Year-round Training

The most efficient way for you as a basketball player to reach maximum levels of strength at a particular point in time is to divide your training year into cycles. This technique is based on incorporating different weights, repetition schemes, set sequences, and training intensities into your workout regimen that allow you to peak in strength for the beginning of team practice in the fall and maintain that strength throughout the entire season.

The most effective method for developing and then maintaining your strength when you most need it is to adhere to a three-cycle system, which includes off-season, pre-season, and in-season training programs. Within each cycle, several mini-cycles exist that are designed to boost your strength in a progressive manner. The workout regimens for these three training cycles, as well as for the mini-cycles within each phase, are outlined in the following three sections. In addition, the training loads, repetition schemes, and training objectives are discussed.

Off-Season Program

□ *Mini-Cycle #1:* April 15–May 15

Load: Light

Repetition Scheme: 12–15

Objective: During your first month back in the weight room, you need to become accustomed to progressive resistance training again. Or, if you have not strength trained before, you need to learn the basics of working out with weights. During the last week of this mini-cycle, you should begin to get a feel for your strength level, using a 12-repetition maximum on all multi-joint lifts.

□ *Mini-Cycle #2:* May 16–June 23

Load: Medium/Heavy

Repetition Scheme: 6–10

Objective: By this time, you should be thoroughly familiar with the exercises you will be using and how to do them correctly. Building a base of strength and developing muscle tolerance are the primary purposes of off-season mini-cycle #2. Focusing intently on these two objectives will help prepare your body for the heavier resistance to come in off-season mini-cycle #3.

Week Off: June 24–June 30

☐ *Mini-Cycle #3:* July 1–August 8

Load: Heavy

Repetition Scheme: 3–7

Objective: The concentration during this mini-cycle is on heavy training. Longer rest periods (e.g., three to four minutes) between sets will be incorporated, and because of the heavy weights used, your total sets will be kept to a minimum. Although your training load will be extremely heavy, it is still critical that you maintain proper exercise form. A tendency always exists to get sloppy with execution as the level of resistance increases. Remember that poor form will slow your progress, and inevitably lead to injury.

Week Off: August 9–August 14

Sample Off-Season Workouts

Tables 8-1 to 8-12 illustrate examples of off-season workouts. It should be noted that the "total sets" figure for each workout does not include warm-up sets.

Exercise:	Sets and Repetitions:
Bench Press	1 x 15, 2 x 12, 1 x 15
Incline Dumbbell Press	1 x 15, 1 x 12, 1 x 15
Shoulder Press	1 x 15, 2 x 12
Machine Fly	2 x 15
Lateral Raise	2 x 15
Straight-Legged Dead Lift	1 x 15, 2 x 12, 1 x 15
Lying Triceps Extension	1 x 15, 1 x 12, 1 x 15
Total Sets: 21	

Table 8-1. Off-season mini-cycle 1: Workout #1 (emphasis chest)

Exercise:	Sets and Repetitions:
Squat	1 x 15, 2 x 12, 1 x 15
Pulldown Behind Neck	1 x 15, 2 x 12, 1 x 15
Lunge	3 x 15
Seated Cable Row	1 x 15, 1 x 12, 1 x 15
Barbell Curl	1 x 15, 1 x 12, 1 x 15
Hammer Curl	2 x 15
Total Sets: 19	

Table 8-2. Off-season mini-cycle 1: Workout #2 (emphasis hips/quadriceps)

Exercise:	Sets and Repetitions:
Incline Press	1 x 15, 2 x 12, 1 x 15
Upright Row	1 x 15, 1 x 12, 1 x 15
Straight-Legged Dead Lift	3 x 15
Dumbbell Shoulder Press	1 x 15, 1 x 12,1 x 15
Leg Curl	1 x 15, 2 x 12, 1 x 15
Bent Lateral Raise	2 x 15
Dip	2 x failure
Total Sets: 21	

Table 8-3. Off-season mini-cycle 1: Workout #1 (emphasis shoulders/hamstrings)

Exercise:	Sets and Repetitions:
Dumbbell Row	1 x 15, 1 x 12, 1 x 15
Machine Pullover	2 x 15
Leg Press	3 x 15
Pulldown to Front	3 x 15
Leg Extension	3 x 15
Preacher Curl	3 x 12
Incline Curl	2 x 15
Total Sets: 19	

Table 8-4. Off-season mini-cycle 1: Workout #2 (emphasis upper back)

Exercise:	Sets and Repetitions:
Incline Press	1 x 10, 1 x 8, 1 x 6, 1 x 10
Dumbbell Bench Press	1 x 10, 1 x 8, 1 x 10
Upright Row	1 x 10, 1 x 6, 1 x 8
Dip (weighted)	1 x 10, 2 x 8
Leg Curl	1 x 10, 2 x 8, 1 x 10
Machine Lateral Raise	1 x 10, 1 x 8
Hyperextension	2 x 10
Dumbbell Triceps Extension	2 x 8
Total Sets: 23	

Table 8-5. Off-season mini-cycle 2: Workout #1 (emphasis chest)

Exercise:	Sets and Repetitions:
Lunge	1 x 10, 2 x 8, 1 x 10
Leg Press	1 x 10, 1 x 6, 2 x 8
Chin-Up	1 x 10, 2 x 8, 1 x 10
Seated Cable Row	1 x 10, 1 x 8, 1 x 10
Preacher Curl	1 x 10, 1 x 8, 1 x 10
Incline Curl	2 x 10
Total Sets: 20	

Table 8-6. Off-season mini-cycle 2: Workout #2 (emphasis hips/quadriceps)

Exercise:	Sets and Repetitions:
Straight-Legged Dead Lifts	1 x 10, 2 x 8, 1 x 10
Bench Press	1 x 10, 1 x 8, 1 x 6, 1 x 10
Push Press	1 x 10, 2 x 6, 1 x 8
Leg Curl	1 x 10, 1 x 8, 1 x 10
Dumbbell Shrugs	1 x 10, 2 x 6, 1 x 8
Lying Triceps Extension	3 x 8
Total Sets: 22	

Table 8-7. Off-season mini-cycle 2: Workout #1 (emphasis shoulders/hamstrings)

Exercise:	Sets and Repetitions:
Pulldown Behind Neck	1 x 10, 1 x 8, 1 x 10
T-Bar Row	1 x 10, 2 x 6, 1 x 8
Squat	1 x 10, 1 x 8, 1 x 6, 1 x 10
Close-Grip Chin-Up (underhand)	2 x 10
Barbell Curl	1 x 10, 1 x 6, 1 x 8
Leg Extension	2 x 10
Hammer Curl	2 x 10
Total Sets: 20	

Table 8-8. Off-season mini-cycle 2: Workout #2 (emphasis upper back)

Exercise:	Sets and Repetitions:
Bench Press	1 x 7, 1 x 5, 1 x 3, 1 x 5
Incline Dumbbell Press	1 x 6, 1 x 4, 1 x 5
Upright Row	1 x 7, 1 x 4, 1 x 6
Lateral Raise	2 x 6
Straight-Legged Dead Lift	3 x 6
Standing Leg Curl	2 x 7
Triceps Press-down	2 x 7
Total Sets: 19	

Table 8-9. Off-season mini-cycle 3: Workout #1 (emphasis chest)

Exercise:	Sets and Repetitions:
Leg Press	1 x 7, 2 x 4, 1 x 5
Lunge	3 x 6
Chin-Up (weighted)	1 x 7, 1 x 5, 1 x 6
Dumbbell Row	1 x 6, 1 x 4, 1 x 5
Leg Extension	1 x 6
Preacher Curl	1 x 6, 1 x 5, 1 x 7
Standing Dumbbell Curl	2 x 6
Total Sets: 19	

Table 8-10. Off-season mini-cycle 3: Workout #2 (emphasis hips/quadriceps)

Exercise:	Sets and Repetitions:
Straight-Legged Dead Lift	1 x 7, 2 x 6, 1 x 7
Incline Press	1 x 6, 1 x 3, 1 x 5
Shoulder Press	1 x 6, 1 x 3, 1 x 7
Leg Curl	3 x 6
Barbell Shrug	2 x 6
Dip (weighted)	2 x 5
Bent Lateral Raise	2 x 7
Total Sets: 19	

Table 8-11. Off-season mini-cycle 3: Workout #1 (emphasis shoulders/hamstrings)

Exercise:	Sets and Repetitions:
Pulldown to Front	1 x 7, 1 x 4, 1 x 5
Machine Row	1 x 7, 1 x 4, 1 x 5, 1 x 6
Squat	1 x 7, 2 x 5, 1 x 6
Leg Extension	2 x 6
Chin-Up (weighted)	2 x 6
Barbell Curl	3 x 6
Total Sets: 18	

Table 8-12. Off-season mini-cycle 3: Workout #2 (emphasis upper back)

Pre-Season Program

☐ *Mini-Cycle #1:* August 15–September 28

Load: As heavy as possible, while incorporating high-intensity techniques.

Repetition Scheme: Low, medium, or high, depending upon the high intensity method used.

Objective: At this time of year, the excitement level of most players is high in anticipation of the upcoming season. It is also the time you will be incorporating the high-intensity strength training techniques that were previously reviewed in chapter 6. These methods will help you blast through strength plateaus and reach your full potential. At least one major muscle group (legs/hips, upper back, chest, and shoulders) will be trained with various high-intensity techniques each workout.

Because of the increased emphasis on basketball skill work and other forms of conditioning (anaerobic training, plyometrics, agility work, etc.), you will find yourself spending less time in the weight room than in the off-season. Less time spent weight training should not mean less strength gains, however. You should take advantage of techniques like super sets, forced repetitions, and rest/pause training to achieve maximum results.

☐ *Mini-Cycle #2:* September 29–October 13

Load: Very heavy

Repetition Scheme: 3 – 6

Objective: Ideally, you will be at your strongest in all lifts during this brief mini-cycle. This is the time to test your strength and evaluate how much improvement you've made since the spring. The workouts will be similar to the sessions you performed in off-season mini-cycle #3, with low repetitions, long rest periods between sets, and limited sets per body part. But hopefully, after working with the high-intensity methods in the previous mini-cycle, you will be handling more weight.

Sample Pre-Season Workouts

Tables 8-13 to 8-20 illustrate sample pre-season workouts. It should be noted that the figure for total sets does not include warm-up sets.

Exercise:	Sets and Repetitions:
Dumbbell Fly } super set	1 x 10, 2 x 8
Bench Press	1 x 8, 2 x 6
Incline DB Press (negative only)	1 x 6, 1 x 4, 1 x 5
Leg Curl	4 x 8
Lateral Raise	4 x 8
Triceps Press-down	2x10
Hyperextension (weighted)	2x10
Total Sets: 21	

Table 8-13. Pre-season mini-cycle 1: Workout #1 (emphasis chest)

Exercise:	Sets and Repetitions:
Leg Press (forced repetitions)	1 x 8 + 4, 1 x 6 + 3, 1 x 5 + 3, 1 x 7 + 4
Step-Up (stripping)	1 x 10, 1 x 8 + 5 + 3, 1 x 10 + 4 + 3
T-Bar Row	1 x 10, 1 x 8, 1 x 6, 1 x 7
Pulldown Behind Neck	1 x 10, 2 x 8
Incline Curl	1 x 10, 2 x 6, 1 x 8
Total Sets: 18	

Table 8-14. Pre-season mini-cycle 1: Workout #2 (emphasis hips/quadriceps)

Exercise:	Sets and Repetitions:
Leg Curl ⎫ super set	1 x 10, 1 x 7, 1 x 8
Straight-Legged DL ⎭	1 x 8, 1 x 6, 1 x 8
Incline Press	1 x 8, 2 x 6, 1 x 8
Lateral Raise ⎫ super set	1 x 10, 2 x 8
Dumbbell Press ⎭	1 x 8, 2 x 6
Upright Row (rest/pause)	1 x 6 + 3 + 3, 1 x 5 + 3 + 2
Close-Grip Bench Press	2 x 8
Total Sets: 20	

Table 8-15. Pre-season mini-cycle 1: Workout #1 (emphasis shoulders/hamstrings)

Exercise:	Sets and Repetitions:
Machine Pullover ⎫ super set	1 x 10, 1 x 8, 1 x 10
Pulldown to Front ⎭	1 x 8, 2 x 6
Lunge	1 x 10, 2 x 8, 1 x 10
Seated Cable Row (super slow)	1 x 8, 1 x 10
Leg Extension	2 x 10
Chin-Up (underhand)	1 x failure
Barbell Curl	1 x 10, 2 x 6, 1 x 8
Total Sets: 19	

Table 8-16. Pre-season mini-cycle 1: Workout #2 (emphasis upper back)

Exercise:	Sets and Repetitions:
Bench Press	1 x 6, 1 x 4, 1 x 3, 1 x 5
Machine Incline Press	1 x 6, 1 x 3, 1 x 5
Straight-Legged Dead Lift	1 x 6, 2 x 5, 1 x 6
Dumbbell Shrug	1 x 6, 1 x 4, 1 x 5
Push Press	2 x 5
Seated Triceps Extension	3 x 6
Total Sets: 19	

Table 8-17. Pre-season mini-cycle 2: Workout #1 (emphasis chest)

Exercise:	Sets and Repetitions:
Squat	1 x 6, 2 x 4, 1 x 6
Lunge	1 x 6, 1 x 5, 1 x 6
Dumbbell Row	1 x 6, 1 x 3, 1 x 5
Leg Extension	1 x 6
Chin-Up (weighted)	1 x 6, 1 x 4, 1 x 5, 1 x 6
Seated Dumbbell Curl	3 x 6
Total Sets: 18	

Table 8-18. Pre-season mini-cycle 2: Workout #2 (emphasis hips/quadriceps)

Exercise:	Sets and Repetitions:
Incline Press	1 x 6, 1 x 3, 1 x 5
Straight-Legged Dead Lift	1 x 6, 2 x 5, 1 x 6
Barbell Shoulder Press	1 x 6, 1 x 4, 1 x 6
Upright Row	1 x 6, 1 x 4, 1 x 5
Dip (weighted)	2 x 6
Leg Curl	2 x 6
Bent Lateral Raise	1 x 6
Total Sets: 18	

Table 8-19. Pre-season mini-cycle 2: Workout #1 (emphasis shoulders/hamstrings)

Exercise:	Sets and Repetitions:
Dumbbell Pullover	2 x 6
Pulldown to Front	3 x 6
Step-Up	1 x 6, 1 x 4, 1 x 5, 1 x 6
T-Bar Row	1 x 6, 1 x 3, 1 x 5
Leg Extension	2 x 6
Preacher Curl	2 x 6
Incline Curl	2 x 6
Total Sets: 18	

Table 8-20. Pre-season mini-cycle 2: Workout #2 (emphasis upper back)

In-Season Program

☐ *Mini-Cycle #1:* October 16 – Beginning of regular-season game play

Load: Medium/heavy

Repetition Scheme: 6 – 10

Objective: The good news concerning this four-to-six week period is that you will have the time to strength train regularly after practice. The challenging news is team practices in the beginning of the season are extremely intense and competitive, and by the time you hit the weight room, you will most likely be physically drained. It is possible, however, with dedication and focus to maintain your strength, and in some cases, even increase it. The workouts in this mini-cycle generally will last no longer than 45 minutes or so. You should train as heavy as your energy level allows, using no high-intensity methods. On days when no team practice is scheduled, longer, more intense strength training sessions can be implemented.

☐ *Mini-Cycle #2:* From the start of regular-season play until the end of the season.

Load: Medium

Repetition: 8 – 12

Objective: The goal of in-season mini-cycle #2 can be described in one word—maintenance. Because of games, practices, travel, school, along with numerous other obligations and responsibilities in your life, it is virtually impossible to make gains in strength during this time of year. But with a strong commitment and skillful time management, you can preserve the strength you've developed in the off-season and pre-season. Most basketball players become somewhat deconditioned during a long, grueling season. Adhering to the strength training programs that are presented in this chapter can help you reverse this process, and can enable you to sustain peak levels of strength, conditioning, and performance.

The following examples outline some suggestions that you can adopt to help you maintain your strength throughout the competitive season:

- *Use multi-joint exercises.* Since your energy and time will be limited, you should stick almost exclusively with multi-joint movements during this time of year. As previously mentioned, multi-joint exercises are the most efficient way to train since they work a number of muscles at once.

- *Strength train immediately following games.* If you have access to the appropriate facilities, strength training after games is a fantastic way to keep current with your routine. Working out after games also helps cool your body down after intense exertion. Post-game workouts should be brief, and large amounts of fluids must be consumed before, during, and after the session. It is imperative that you respect your energy level after competition, along with monitoring any injuries you may have sustained during the game.

- *Use off days constructively.* As any athlete can attest, off days during the competitive season are precious commodities. A free day provides a basketball player with an excellent opportunity to hit the weights hard. In my college playing days at Duke University, I used the four-or-five day break from practice during the Christmas holidays to focus primarily on strength training. In fact, the only time I touched a basketball over the break was for a few minutes of shooting and ballhandling after my weight workouts. Because of this factor, I always felt strong and energized heading into Atlantic Coast Conference play in January. So, if you have the energy and do not have a game the following day, plan on strength training hard on your days off from practice.

- *Schedule a team-strength workout instead of practice.* It is ultimately up to your coach of course, but having a team strength-training session, in lieu of practice, can accomplish a great deal. Along with allowing players to stay up with their programs, it provides everyone–players, coaches, trainers, and even managers–a mental break from the monotony of regular practice.

- *Strength train consistently in the off-season.* Perhaps the best way to ensure that you remain strong throughout the long basketball season is to commit yourself to working consistently hard in the weight room in the off-season. The more strength you build in the off-season, the easier it will be maintain your level of peak performance when it counts—during the competitive campaign.

While reasonably intense leg training is recommended during the season, you must take care not to overdo it. As almost every basketball player is aware, playing basketball puts tremendous stress on your legs. No sport involves more running, jumping, cutting, and sliding. As a result, too much weight training can tire your legs to the point where your on-court performance suffers.

The key to successful in-season leg training is mind/body awareness. You must be acutely aware of how your legs respond to various training loads, and then proceed to adjust your routine accordingly. Of course, this point is easier said than done. In reality, it takes considerable time and concentration to develop this intuitive feel for your training. An approach I have often used is to encourage athletes to carefully monitor how their legs feel after training at different intensities during the off-season cycle and then to translate that knowledge to the season. This approach gives them a realistic indication of how much their bodies can tolerate in terms of leg training. As was discussed previously in this book, recuperation from workouts is a very personal matter. Some basketball players are able to recover very quickly and can exercise their legs with weights all season at a fairly high level of intensity without becoming overtrained. Other athletes recover slowly, and tend to perform better on the court when they're doing very little direct leg work during the season.

Sample In-Season Workouts

Exercise:	Sets and Repetitions:
Bench Press	1 x 10, 2 x 6, 1 x 8
Incline Press	1 x 10, 1 x 6, 1 x 8
Leg Curl	1 x 10, 2 x 8, 1 x 10
Upright Row	1 x 8, 1 x 6, 1 x 8
Lateral Raise	2 x 10
Dip (weighted)	1 x 10, 2 x 8
Total Sets: 19	

Table 8-21. In-season mini-cycle 1: Workout #1 (emphasis chest)

Exercise:	Sets and Repetitions:
Leg Press	1 x 10, 2 x 6, 1 x 8
Chin-Up (weighted)	1 x 10, 1 x 6, 1 x 8
Step-Up	3 x 8
Dumbbell Row	3 x 8
Barbell Curl	1 x 10, 2 x 8
Leg Extension	1 x 10
Total Sets: 17	

Table 8-22. In-season mini-cycle 1: Workout #2 (emphasis hips/quadriceps)

Exercise:	Sets and Repetitions:
Incline Dumbbell Press	1 x 10, 2 x 6, 1 x 8
Straight-Legged Dead Lift	1 x 10, 2 x 8, 1 x 10
Shoulder Press	4 x 8
Bent Lateral Raise	3 x 10
Standing Leg Curl	2 x 10
Triceps Press-down	2 x 8
Total Sets: 19	

Table 8-23. In-season mini-cycle 1: Workout #1 (emphasis shoulders/hamstrings)

Exercise:	Sets and Repetitions:
Machine Pullover	3 x 10
Pulldown to Back	1 x 8, 1 x 6, 1 x 8
Squat	1 x 10, 1 x 8, 1 x 6, 1 x 10
Seated Cable Row	1 x 10, 1 x 6, 1 x 8
Lunge	2 x 10
Incline Curl	3 x 8
Total Sets: 18	

Table 8-24. In-season mini-cycle 1: Workout #2 (emphasis upper back)

Exercise:	Sets and Repetitions:
Bench Press	1 x 12, 2 x 8, 1 x 10
Machine Incline Press	3 x 10
Leg Curl	1 x 12, 2 x 8, 1 x 10
Push Press	1 x 10, 1 x 8, 1 x 12
Shrug	2 x 10
Dip	1 x failure
Total Sets: 17	

Table 8-25. In-season mini-cycle 2: Workout #1 (emphasis chest)

Exercise:	Sets and Repetitions:
Leg Press	1 x 12, 2 x 8, 1 x 10
Chin-Up	4 x failure
Lunge`	3 x 12
T-Bar Row	1 x 10, 2 x 8
Barbell Curl	1 x 10, 1 x 8, 1 x 10
Total Sets: 17	

Table 8-26. In-season mini-cycle 2: Workout #2 (emphasis hips/quadriceps)

Exercise:	Sets and Repetitions:
Straight-Legged Dead Lift	1 x 12, 1 x 10, 1 x 12
Incline Press	1 x 10, 1 x 8, 1 x 12
Upright Row	3 x 10
Machine Lateral Raise	1 x 12, 1 x 10, 1 x 12
Leg Curl	3 x 10
Machine Fly	2 x 10
Total Sets: 17	

Table 8-27. In-season mini-cycle 2: Workout #1 (emphasis shoulders/hamstrings)

Exercise:	Sets and Repetitions:
Seated Cable Row	4 x 10
Pulldown to Front	1 x 10, 1 x 8, 1 x 10
Lunge	3 x 12
Chin-Up (underhand)	2 x failure
Step-Up	1 x 12, 1 x 8, 1 x 10
Preacher Curl	2 x 10
Total Sets: 17	

Table 8-28. In-season mini-cycle 2: Workout #2 (emphasis upper back)

Abdominal Workout

Exercise:	Sets and Repetitions:
Legs-in-the-Air Sit-Ups	2 x 200, weight added x 100, weight added x 75, 2 x 100
Side Sit-Up	2 x 150 each side
Bench Crunches	2 x 150, weight added x 75
Hanging Leg Raise	3 x failure
Total Sets: 11	

Table 8-29. Year-round, sample abdominal workout.

Abdominal Workout Guidelines

▸ Abdominal workouts should be performed four to five days a week, either on workout or non-workout days.

▸ To add weight to sit-ups or crunches, most trainers grasp a dumbbell or a barbell plate behind their heads. A medicine ball may also be used.

▸ When exercising your abdominal muscles, it is best to focus on the lower portion during the majority of your sets.

▸ When training the midsection, it is extremely important to breathe freely and deeply, because breathing tends to constrict during abdominal exercise.

Strength Training Log

Date:	Day:	Time of Day:
Cycle:	Workout:	Rest Between Sets:
Total Sets:	Workout Time:	

Exercise/Weight/Reps	Exercise/Weight/Sets

Additional Comments

Table 8-30. Sample strength training log.

PART IV
MOVEMENT TRAINING
FOR BASKETBALL

CHAPTER 9

Plyometrics

Plyometrics, or "jump training" as it was originally known in Europe, has experienced tremendous popularity in the past decade within the sports-conditioning community. This method of training includes a series of jumps, hops, bounds, and other explosive athletic movements that are designed to enable a muscle to achieve maximal force in the least amount of time. In essence, plyometrics link the speed of movement with strength to produce power by stretching or loading the muscles as fast as possible prior to a forceful contraction.

Plyometric training has its share of staunch proponents who feel it is the ultimate performance-enhancing tool that has ever been developed for athletes. It also has a smattering of detractors who believe it is dangerous and mostly a well-hyped fraud. Obviously, both ends of this argument are extreme to say the least. Like most reasonable basketball-conditioning specialists, I have always tried to stay clear of the fray and draw my own conclusions concerning plyometric training.

What You Can Expect from Plyometrics

Let's start with some cold hard facts: plyometrics will not work miracles. It will not, as some advertisers claim, turn you into a skywalker overnight. Furthermore, it has a certain degree of injury risk, especially if engaged in too frequently, executed improperly, or performed by unfit individuals. As such, plyometric training is not for everyone.

Before you turn to the next section and vow to stay clear of plyometric training forever, consider a little positive news on the subject. Many athletes competing in explosive-type sports, most prominently track and field competitors, have shown tangible results by using plyometrics as part of their improvement programs. Sprinters have lowered their times, high jumpers have raised their jump heights, and shot putters have increased their throwing distances—all (allegedly) because of plyometrics. Basketball players, in my opinion, can benefit in a similar fashion. Plyometrics, if approached intelligently and incorporated in conjunction with a year-round weight training program and regular flexibility work, can help a basketball player increase his quickness, jumping ability, and level of explosiveness that will translate into improved performance on the court.

Developing Your Plyometric Training Program

A number of factors should be weighed when designing a plyometric training program for basketball, including the following:

Equipment

Although many plyometric drills can be performed without equipment, there are a few basic accessories with which you should be familiar, including:

- *Barriers.* Barriers are used in many plyometric drills. Their height can vary from as low as six inches to as high as two feet or more, depending on the nature of the drill and the athletic ability of the practitioner. The safest barriers are made of foam padding. The simplest barriers are plastic cones.

- *Boxes.* Boxes used for plyometrics must be sturdy, have semi-soft, nonslip landing surfaces, and can range in height from a few inches to three feet. The top of the box should measure a minimum of 18 by 24 inches. Due to the recent popularity of plyometrics, some fitness stores now sell specialized plyometrics boxes.

- *Medicine balls.* Medicine balls have been around for decades. Originally, they were used extensively by boxers in their fight preparation. These balls are weighted objects used mostly for upper-body plyometric work and abdominal training. Rubber medicine balls are recommended because they are easily gripped, bounce evenly when they hit the floor, and come in an assortment of weights.

Training Surface

Plyometric training can be performed on any reasonably soft surface. Wood gym floors, low-cut grass, and rubberized tracks are fine. Exercising on hard surfaces and uneven terrain should be avoided.

Footwear

Because plyometric exercises are high-impact exercises, it is essential that you wear proper shoes during your training sessions in order to prevent injury. High-topped basketball shoes are best because they provide reliable lateral support, are sufficiently cushioned for landing after jumps, and have nonslip soles. Running or jogging shoes lack lateral stability and using them for plyometrics will leave you susceptible to twisted ankles and knees. As such, they should not be worn while performing plyometrics. Furthermore, engaging in plyometrics barefoot is also not recommended.

Schedule Description

Program Length

A plyometrics program for basketball should encompass 12 consecutive weeks of workouts beginning in mid-July and terminating just before the start of fall practice.

Number of Workouts Per Week

Because of the demanding nature of plyometric training, no more than two workouts per week should be scheduled. The individual sessions should be separated by a minimum of 48 hours and preferably 72 hours.

Sets and Repetitions

Similar to strength training, sets and repetitions for plyometric workouts will vary with the athlete's needs, level of fitness, experience with plyometrics, and the time of year. Typically, a total of 100 to 200 contacts (repetitions) per workout should occur. For best results, spread the repetitions among three to four different plyometric drills. Three to six sets per drill are recommended. The repetition range per set is usually six to ten.

Rest Between Sets

The rest periods between sets of plyometric exercises are mostly determined by the level of intensity at which you are training. For warm-up movements and low-intensity work, one-to two-minute rest intervals are sufficient. High-intensity efforts require up to four minutes recovery time between sets.

Workout Duration

Plyometric workouts should generally range between 20 and 45 minutes. Shorter sessions may be appropriate for younger ballplayers and for athletes coming off injuries or extended layoffs. Engaging in plyometric training for longer than 45 minutes is not recommended.

In-Season Plyometrics

Basketball players should use plyometrics sparingly during the competitive campaign. Because of the grueling nature of the season, most athletes will not have the energy to make plyometrics worthwhile. The only exceptions would be for players not receiving much playing time or if the schedule allows for a prolonged break such as during the Christmas holidays.

Keys to Safe and Productive Plyometric Workouts

Preparation

Proper preparation is perhaps the most important factor to successful, injury-free plyometric workouts. Engaging in plyometric training (or any intense physical activity for that matter) without a solid strength and conditioning foundation is a major mistake, one that will likely lead to frustration and injury.

Athletes must have a minimum of ten weeks of weight-room strength training behind them prior to embarking on a plyometrics program. Lower-body strength work is most important. Conventional guidelines suggest that athletes should be able to squat 1.5 to 2 times their body weight and/or leg press 2.5 times their body weight before beginning intense plyometric workouts. Keep in mind, these are just averages and attaining the aforementioned weight-to-body-weight ratios is not absolutely essential to starting with plyometrics, provided you are healthy and progressing consistently with your strength training program. Along with a solid strength base, it is also important that you have a reasonable measure of flexibility and a satisfactory level of aerobic and anaerobic fitness before participating in plyometric training sessions.

Learn Proper Execution

Performing plyometric drills correctly is essential to safe and effective workouts. The high-impact and high-intensity nature of plyometric movements requires you to pay close attention to execution or risk injury. For best results, perform your first few training sessions at half speed, focusing on technique and form, rather then velocity and intensity. In a relatively short time, as you become comfortable with the drills in your program, full-speed, all-out efforts can commence.

Use Basketball-Related Movements

In order to maximize your plyometric training, it is imperative that you use basketball-specific movements. The drills detailed at the end of this chapter are a good start, but they provide only a sampling of the many exercises at your disposal. There are virtually hundreds of available plyometric drills from which to choose. You are strongly encouraged to research other sources for additional exercises that pertain to basketball. When you become stronger and more comfortable with plyometrics, feel free to develop your own basketball-specific drills. Learning and creating a variety of movements will make your training more interesting and, ultimately, more successful.

Warm-up and Cool-down Sufficiently

Plyometric training, similar to all conditioning disciplines, requires a full warm-up and cool-down. Refer to chapter 1 for detailed information concerning warm-up, cool-down, and flexibility training.

Progression

Once proper technique is mastered, you should, at your own pace, progress from simpler plyometrics movements to the more complicated variety. An example of a simple plyometric movement would be standing rim jumps, while a complicated plyometric movement might be lateral box jumps. Always begin your workouts with simple movements.

Effort and Intensity

Plyometric exercises are designed to be performed at a high level of intensity. Once your warm-ups are concluded, it is critical that every set of your workout is executed with an all-out effort.

Who Should Not Use Plyometrics

Although plyometric training is recommended for most basketball players, there are some individuals who should avoid plyometrics. The following three situations illustrate instances where athletes should not engage in plyometrics.

- *Pre-adolescents.* Pre-adolescent athletes, unless extremely physically mature, should refrain from plyometrics. The risk of injury to muscles, bones, and joints is substantially higher prior to puberty than it is afterward. Young ballplayers would be better served using their time and energy working on basketball skills and general conditioning rather than experimenting with advanced high-impact training methods like plyometrics.

- *Large athletes.* Large athletes (i.e., those individuals weighing more than 225 pounds) must take great care when performing plyometrics. Some may want to skip this particular conditioning technique altogether. The force of most landings during plyometric drills is intense, and larger ballplayers are much more susceptible to injury than their smaller counterparts. If, as a bigger athlete, you wish to engage in plyometrics, I suggest you only use general movements such as front cone hops, standing rim jumps, and double leg jumps. All box jumps should be avoided. No exceptions!

- *Injured athletes.* Obviously, any athlete who is injured should not engage in plyometric training. Also, individuals with a history of lower-body injuries should abstain from plyometrics unless they're cleared by a physician.

Plyometric Drills

Drill: Rim Touches

Execution: Facing a basketball rim or other elevated object, such as a cross bar, assume an erect stance, with your head up and your eyes aimed at the rim. Proceed by bending quickly to the jumping position (approximately three-quarters to parallel) and instantaneously explode upward toward the target, reaching up with one hand and attempt to touch the rim. Repeat for the required number of repetitions, always focusing on popping off the ground as quickly as possible.

Drill: Double Leg Jumps

Execution: Assume an erect stance with your head straight and your eyes focused in front of you. Continue by bending quickly into the jumping position (approximately three-quarters to parallel) and immediately explode straight up as high as possible, while concurrently pulling your knees toward your chest. During the jump phase of the drill, your arms should be straight out in front of you. Similar to rim jumps, your goal is to quickly jump as high as you can each time. Perform the required number of repetitions.

Drill: Front Jumps

Execution: Line up three to eight hurdles (barriers, cones, boxes, etc.), spaced two to five feet apart. The height of the hurdles will vary from six inches to one foot or so, depending on your athletic ability, strength, and experience with plyometrics. Stand facing the hurdles with your feet shoulder-width apart and your knees flexed. Jump over each hurdle, concentrating on spending as little time as possible on the ground. After you've jumped over the last hurdle, turn 180 degrees, and retrace your jumps to the starting position. Repeat for the required number of repetitions.

Drill: Lateral Jumps

Execution: Line up three hurdles (barriers, cones, boxes, etc.) spaced two to three feet apart. The hurdles you use will range in height from a few inches up to two feet, depending on your athletic ability, strength, and experience with plyometrics. Start with your knees flexed and your feet shoulder-width apart and parallel to the first hurdle. Jump sideways over the line of hurdles, focusing on leaving your feet quickly after each landing. After you've jumped over the last hurdle, immediately retrace your jumps back to the starting position. Repeat for the required number of repetitions.

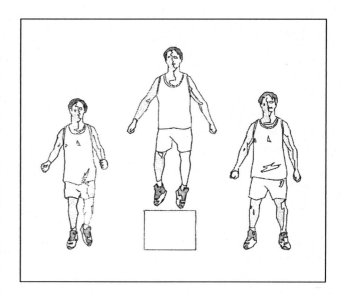

Drill: Front Box Jumps

Execution: Stand facing a box, with your knees flexed, your feet shoulder-width apart, and your hands clasped behind your head (optional). The height of the box will measure from one to three feet, depending on your athletic ability, strength, and experience with plyometrics. Jump up onto the box, hop down, and then immediately upon landing, jump back up (one repetition). Repeat for the required number of repetitions.

Drill: Side Box Jumps

Execution: Stand with your knees flexed and your feet shoulder-width apart at the side of a box. Similar to front box jumps, the box can measure anywhere from one to three feet depending on your athletic ability, strength, and experience with plyometrics. Jump up onto the box and back down to the ground to the starting position. Repeat for the required number of repetitions.

Drill: Overhead Toss

Execution: Stand with your knees slightly flexed and your feet close together, holding an appropriately weighted medicine ball overhead. Step forward under control and release the ball powerfully at approximately head height. Repeat with a partner for the required number of repetitions.

Drill: Backward Toss

Execution: Stand with your knees bent and your feet slightly wider than shoulder-width apart and pick up an appropriately weighted medicine ball from the ground. Proceed by throwing the ball up over your head as far as possible toward your partner. Repeat with your partner for the required number of repetitions.

CHAPTER 10

Speed, Quickness, and Agility

Speed Training

Unlike the often stated basketball announcer's claim that, "You can't teach height," the traditional track coach's adage, "Sprinters are born, not made," is not entirely accurate. While genetics certainly plays the major role in an individual's potential running speed, and the fact that the vast majority of the individuals who will read this book will never run as fast as Maurice Green, Allen Iverson, or Marshall Faulk, certain training methods exist that can help you increase your sprinting speed considerably.

Keys to Efficient Sprinting

Conditioning

The first step to reaching your speed potential is to achieve good physical condition. Without going into detail here (the rest of the book does that), this step includes developing a solid strength base, especially in the lower body, establishing satisfactory aerobic and anaerobic fitness, maintaining optimal body composition—excess body fat will obviously slow you down—and attaining a reasonable level of flexibility.

Running Mechanics

The most important variable in increasing your sprinting speed involves improving your running mechanics. Although every individual has a unique running style, there are many fundamental sprint-enhancing practices that all athletes can follow to improve their running form.

With regard to running mechanics, the two major factors in how fast you run can be described by a simple equation: stride length x stride frequency = sprinting speed. Stride length is the space covered in an individual stride. Stride frequency is the time it takes to accomplish a single stride. In order to become a faster sprinter, you must enhance your stride length by intensifying your force against the track or court, while maintaining your balance with your stride frequency. Powerful and efficient arm movement must also be employed.

The following list details some characteristics of effective sprinting:

- Running in a naturally erect position is central to good sprinting technique. Many young athletes have been taught to lean forward when sprinting. This positioning will actually slow you down and can contribute to a loss of balance at high speeds.

- Your head should be up and straight, and your eyes focused toward the destination of the sprint.

- Your arms, shoulders, and hands should be relaxed when sprinting. Many athletes tend to keep their torsos rigid when running at top speed. Remember, in order to sprint fast, you must always remain relaxed.

- Your push-off leg should always end up completely extended, and it is important not to over-stride during your stride cycle. Increasing your stride length by unnaturally forcing your foot to land far ahead of your body actually hinders your sprinting speed.

- Your arm action should come from your shoulders. During the upswing, your hands should reach just in front of your chin and slightly inside your shoulders. On the downswing, your hands should reach no further back than your hips.

- Artificially increasing your stride frequency by trying to move your legs too quickly will make you move fast, but mostly in one place. Traversing the maximum amount of ground in the shortest period of time involves the correct balance of stride length and stride frequency.

- Your elbows should always be kept at a 90-degree angle, forcing all of your arm action to stay close to your body. If your arms are too far from your body when sprinting, it will disrupt your stride rhythm.

- Your torso should remain mostly stationary, and your shoulders must be squared to the direction of the sprint throughout.

Training Methods to Increase Speed

Other than improving your running form and attaining a peak level of physical condition, three additional speed-enhancing methods exist that you may consider incorporating into your off-season conditioning program. The first, acceleration sprinting, entails, as the name suggests, gradually increasing your speed until you reach a full sprint. The second, added resistance sprinting, calls for adding weight or resistance to your frame in order to make the act of sprinting more difficult. The third, overspeed training, increases your stride length and rate by placing higher than normal demands on your nervous system. Similar to plyometrics, overspeed training will cause your neuromuscular system to become accustomed to faster speeds, and therefore enable you to attain those speeds without facilitation. These techniques are demanding and must be implemented cautiously. Too much intense training, as you know, will lead to overtraining and eventually to injury. If you decide to incorporate these techniques into your improvement program, it is best to perform them in lieu of an anaerobic sprint workout (refer to chapter 5).

Acceleration Sprints

As discussed previously, acceleration sprints involve gradually increasing your speed during the course of a run. Typically, when engaging in a 100-yard acceleration sprint, you would start with a jog of about 15 yards, accelerate to a stride for 30 yards, and then proceed to sprinting all-out for 55 yards. Between sprints, walk 60 yards or so, and then repeat the sequence. Many in the track community feel sprinting in this way helps athletes perfect their running form, while at the same time, allowing them to achieve a solid speed workout.

Added Resistance Sprinting

•   *Weighted vests.* The weighted vest has been utilized in sports conditioning for decades. It is used for such diverse purposes as road work for boxers and jump training for beach volleyball players. Sprinting while wearing a weighted vest has shown to be an effective and safe way for athletes to increase speed. This form of training involves several basic guidelines that you should follow, however. First, the weight of the vest should never be heavier than 8 to 10% of your body weight. Subsequently, you should gradually increase the weight of the vest over a period of four or five workouts until you reach your desired vest to body weight ratio.

Second, it is imperative that proper and natural running form be maintained at all times. If the weight of the vest affects your running form, guess what…the vest is too heavy. All factors considered, it is always better to perform your workouts with less weight, than to risk injury by pushing it.

Third, if you suffer from lower-back problems, weighted-vest training is not for you. The additional weight, even if it's only a small percentage of your body weight, can make you more susceptible to a lower-back injury.

Weighted vests can be purchased at most fitness and sporting goods stores. Make sure that the vest you buy is weight adjustable.

• *Harnesses/Parachutes.* Both the two-person harness and the resistance parachute are used frequently by track athletes and have gained popularity in the football community as well—mostly because of the emphasis on the 40-yard dash in evaluating players. Sprinting while wearing a harness has some speed-enhancing benefits. Furthermore, it is generally less taxing to the body than wearing a weighted vest. The basic premise of this type of training is to have one partner hold the handles connected to the harness tightly without giving ground, while the other partner sprints straight ahead pulling the resistance. If a partner is not available, the handles can be fastened to a sturdy object such as a tree or goal post. Your partner should be approximately the same weight as you, for obvious reasons. The resistance parachute, while seemingly high-tech, is basically an overly expensive item that provides no more in the way of speed benefits than either the two-person harness or a weighted vest.

• *Ankle weights/weighted shoes.* Ankle weights were popular for a brief time in the 1970s before research showed speed gains to be minimal by athletes who used them. Moreover, many players complained of knee pain after running and jumping for an extended time while wearing ankle weights. Many in the medical community felt the extra weight distributed on the lower legs unnaturally stretched ligaments in the knee and ankle. Weighted shoes basically are the modern versions of ankle weights and should be strictly avoided.

Overspeed Training

• *Downhill Sprinting.* The most popular form of overspeed training is downhill sprinting. It requires no equipment to speak of, and if you can find a hill with the appropriate decline angle, you're all set. Finding the proper running area is the real challenge. Generally, you should try and locate a 40-yard or so stretch that has an approximate 3-degree downgrade. Anything steeper is not advisable, because it will cause you to compromise your running form and may be dangerous. Downhill sprints of 20 to 30 yards work best for basketball players. As with all forms of intense sprinting, a thorough warm-up should always be performed.

• *Towing.* Towing is perhaps the most effective form of overspeed training available. Many athletes have lowered their sprint times substantially by using this method. The downside to towing is that most individuals and schools do not have access to the necessary equipment for this form of training, such as elastic tubing (other more expensive equipment is available as well). Also, capable oversight by an experienced track and field coach or an athletic conditioning specialist is a must for all workouts.

Towing workouts should always take place on a soft grassy surface, such as a football or soccer field, and involve a towing apparatus, such as the aforementioned elastic tubing. The tubing should measure approximately 20 to 25 feet. It should be fastened to your waist by a belt, while the other end should be connected to a partner or a sturdy object of some kind. After a few warm-up strides, walk backward about 30 yards from where the tubing is attached and proceed to sprint all-out as the tubing snaps back and pulls you forward. It is extremely important that you maintain proper running form during all towing sprints. Also, avoid stretching the tubing too far. Most elastic tubing will stretch five to six times its relaxed length. For safety reasons, check the tubing carefully for any damage prior to your training sessions.

• *High-Intensity Stationary Biking.* Although stationary bikes are predominantly used for aerobic conditioning, many gyms and health clubs now offer interval stationary biking classes that focus on full-speed pedaling. Pedaling at high speeds has been shown to improve sprinting speed to some extent. Preliminary indications suggest that correlating high-speed cycling with the time it would take you to sprint 25 to 30 yards using an overspeed method such as downhill sprinting can be very beneficial. While still recommended as a form of overspeed training, high-intensity, stationary biking is the least effective of the overspeed techniques discussed in this section and should be included with at least one other overspeed method in your training regimen.

Speed Technique Drills

The following exercises are technique drills, and are not meant to be performed at full speed. The premise underlying performing speed-technique drills is to learn proper running form so when you run all-out on the track during anaerobic workouts or in a game while hustling back on defense, your body will automatically remember the speed-promoting movement patterns.

Speed technique drills can be implemented on a year-round basis. In the early off-season, it is best to perform these drills after your aerobic training. Later in the off-season, speed work can be used as a warm-up for your anaerobic workouts. During the competitive season, one speed workout per week accomplished before practice is recommended. Most speed sessions should last about ten minutes.

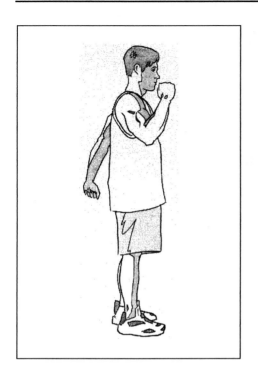

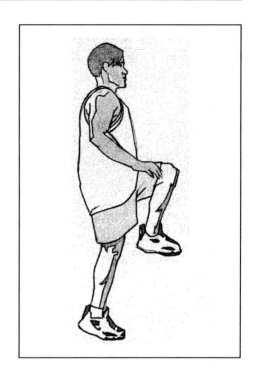

Drill: Arm Motion

Execution: Stand with your knees slightly bent and your legs shoulder-width apart and repetitively swing your arms forward and back as if you were sprinting. Remember to keep your shoulders and hands relaxed and to raise your arms only as high as your chest on the upswing and only as low as your hips on the downswing.

Drill: Ups and Downs

Execution: Accentuating staying on the balls of your feet, bounce your leg into a high-knee position as if you were marching in place. Your back leg should reach full extension. The emphasis should be on lifting your front knee as high as possible. Proper arm action should always be incorporated.

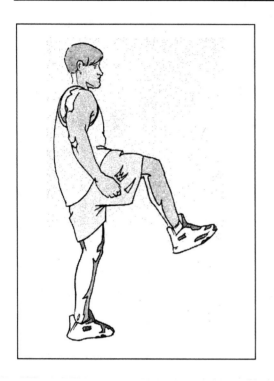

Drill: Leg Pull

Execution: With one leg flat on the ground, extend the other leg out in front of you. Proceed by pulling the extended leg down to the ground in a powerful manner. Repeat the required number of repetitions with both legs.

Drill: Bounding

Execution: Starting with a slow jog, attempt to bound as high as you can into the air, while maintaining a high-knee running action. Emphasize full-extension of your push leg, and as you increase your speed, try to expand the space between bounds. Similar to all sprint-technique drills, correct arm action should be incorporated.

Quickness and Agility Training

The need for quickness is ever present in basketball—quickness to catch a loose ball, quickness on a drive to the basket, quickness in helping out a teammate after he gets beat off the dribble, etc. Almost every trip down the basketball floor involves quick and agile movements from the majority of the participants taking part in the action. It is no surprise that many of the NBA's best players, including Allen Iverson, Steve Francis, Mike Bibby, Jason Kidd, and Kobe Bryant are also among the league's quickest players.

Quickness and agility, more so than straight-ahead running speed, can be increased substantially. A great example of this factor involves former Boston Celtic great Larry Bird. In his playing days, Bird could never sprint up and down the court with the likes of Julius "Dr. J" Erving, Michael Jordan, and Dominique Wilkins, but his quick, instinctive first step, developed through countless hours of hard work, rivaled all three. Many players, both before and after Larry Bird, have improved their quickness and agility by incorporating agility drills similar to the ones documented at the end of this section. Accordingly, follow the agility program prescribed in this chapter and look forward to enhancing your quickness and agility substantially.

Schedule Description

Most basketball players have engaged in some form of agility training, either during team practices or at summer basketball camps. The agility drills prescribed in this chapter focus on improving lateral quickness (a major factor in good defensive play), and on enhancing your ability to start, stop, and change direction quickly and efficiently. Agility workouts should be performed two days per week in the off-season on the same days as your plyometric training (plyometrics and agility training have many common characteristics). Similar to plyometric work, agility training begins in mid-July and ends just before the commencement of fall practice (12 weeks in total).

All agility sessions should be done on a basketball court, and should be performed at high intensity. Table 10-1 presents an overview of the basic parameters for conducting your agility-drill training. It is also important to note that unless otherwise specified, agility training should not be used for conditioning purposes. The focus of your agility workouts should always be on improving quickness, balance, and agility.

- *Program length:* 12 weeks
- *Drills per workout:* 3 to 4
- *Sets:* 6 to 10 per drill
- *Drill duration:* 10 to 15 seconds
- *Rest periods between sets:* 30 to 45 seconds
- *Intensity:* High

Table 10-1. Recommended parameters for agility-drill training.

During the regular season, because most team practices will provide sufficient agility-related exercise, organized agility workouts are, for the most part, not necessary.

Agility Drills

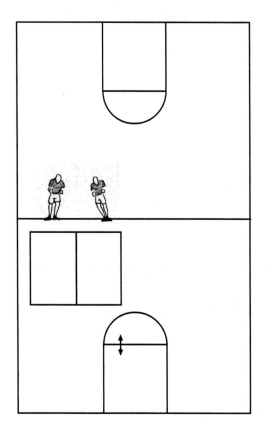

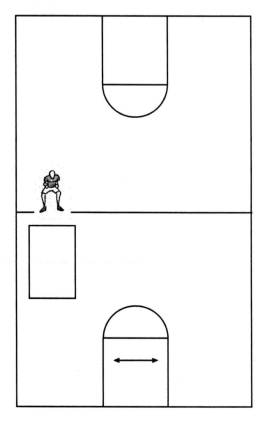

Drill: Quick Feet

Execution: Stand parallel to the foul line or baseline with your feet close together. On command, hop back and forth over the line as fast as possible, keeping your feet together throughout. Continue for ten seconds.

Drill: Lane Slides

Execution: Start in a defensive stance in the middle of the three-second lane. On command, slide back and forth across the lane as fast as possible without crossing your feet. Continue for 10 to 15 seconds.

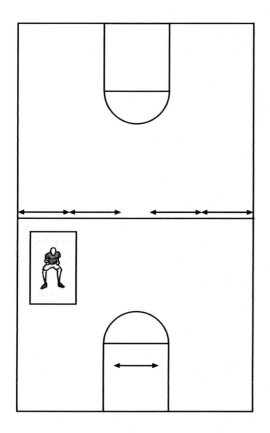

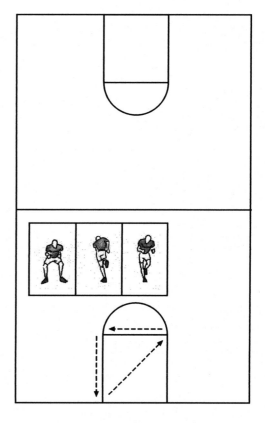

Drill: Slide with Response

Execution: Start in a defensive stance at center court. Have a partner shout "move," and then proceed to slide right or left without crossing your feet. When your partner shouts "move" again, change directions quickly and slide the opposite way. Continue to slide back and forth on response for 15 seconds.

Drill: Sprint, Slide, Backpedal

Execution: Start where the lane line intersects the baseline (on either side). On command, sprint diagonally across the three-second area to where the opposite lane line meets the foul line. Then, immediately slide across the foul line to the opposite lane line. From there, proceed without pausing to backpedal to the starting position. Alternate starting sides for the required number of repetitions.

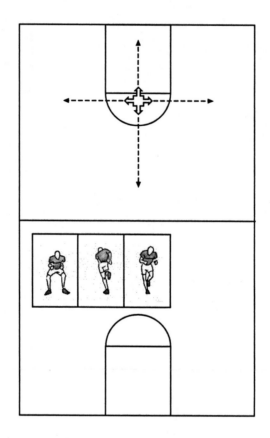

Drill: Change Direction with Response

Execution: Assume a defensive stance at the middle of the foul line, facing center court. Have your partner stand in the center jump circle, facing you. Respond to your partner's direction to either slide left, slide right, backpedal, or sprint straight ahead. This drill should be performed for 10 to 15 seconds. It can, however, be extended for conditioning purposes.

CHAPTER 11

Cross Training Options

Cross training has been a buzzword in fitness circles for many years. This conditioning option entails alternating a variety of exercise choices throughout your training year. Cross training regularly will keep your workouts interesting, help prevent overuse injuries, and assist in heading off fitness plateaus that might otherwise arise. This chapter reviews seven additional training modalities that you should consider incorporating into your basketball conditioning program.

Jumping Rope

Every basketball player should own a jump rope. In fact, every basketball player should own three jump ropes: a light-handled, easy-turning rope; a heavy-handled rope; and a heavy-corded rope. Working out consistently with a variety of jump ropes will help improve every aspect of your basketball conditioning and athleticism. Training with an easy-turning rope can help enhance your level of quickness, footwork, and coordination, and can also improve your level of aerobic conditioning. Jumping with a heavy-handled rope can help improve your hand, wrist, and forearm strength, along with providing a terrific anaerobic workout. Exercising with a heavy-corded rope also affords a superb anaerobic workout, albeit of shorter duration—30 seconds will be the limit for most, and will aid in building strength throughout your upper body, especially in your shoulders. Working with this type of rope can also augment your ability to move quickly and explosively in all directions on the basketball floor.

Jumping rope is a tremendous exercise for all basketball players, but perhaps it is most beneficial for young, developing big players, many of whom have slow feet, poor footwork, and lack coordination. Skipping rope regularly forces young centers and power forwards to make a habit of moving their feet quickly and consistently. It also provides a coordination-enhancing training vehicle that can help them gain confidence in their ever-growing bodies. Combining a year-round rope-jumping program with the requisite honing of low-post moves, skills, and shots can pay great dividends for big players at all levels.

Tips for Effective Jump Rope Workouts

Rope Length

A jump rope should be long enough to reach from armpit to armpit, while passing under both feet. Some basketball players, because of their height, may have difficulty finding a long jump rope at local retail stores. In that case, you should contact a few jump rope manufacturers and see if they can design a rope for you. Some basketball magazines may advertise longer ropes for sale as well.

Turning the Jump Rope

Turning a jump rope is a fairly simple process. It entails turning your hands and wrists in a natural forward circle. Your upper arms are held close to your torso, and your forearms are pointed downward at a 45-degree angle. Your wrists and hands do most of the work when turning a light-handled rope; your forearms come into play when turning a heavy-handled rope; and your shoulder girdle is engaged when turning a heavy-corded rope.

Where to Jump

It is best to conduct your rope-jumping workouts on semi-soft surfaces—wood basketball courts and soft running tracks are ideal. Hard services, such as concrete and asphalt, should be avoided. Most sporting goods and fitness equipment stores sell rubberized pads, which can be placed over hard surfaces during your jump-rope sessions.

Warm Up Lower Legs Thoroughly

Jumping rope can be extremely hard on your lower legs (calves, shins, ankles, and feet). In order to prevent injury and soreness, it is imperative that you warm up and stretch your lower legs thoroughly prior to a rope-jumping workout.

Jumping Patterns

Although there are virtually hundreds of jumping patterns that you can follow when jumping rope, the following three basic methods are all you need to learn in order to enjoy stimulating and productive workouts:

- *Alternate foot jump:* The athlete jumps once each rope turn, alternating between his left foot and right foot. Jumping in this manner resembles running in place.

- *Two-foot jump:* The athlete jumps once each rope turn, with both feet hitting the ground simultaneously. Your feet should be slightly closer than shoulder-width when executing this jumping pattern.

- *Skip jump:* The athlete jumps once each rope turn, alternating in no set sequence between left foot, right foot, and both feet simultaneously.

Uphill Sprinting/Stadium-Step Running

Two of the best alternate methods of conditioning that basketball players can engage in are uphill sprinting and stadium step running. Both modes are used to increase running speed and condition the anaerobic systems.

Uphill sprinting is highly popular with both track athletes (mostly sprinters) and football players, as well as with basketball players. In fact, Jerry Rice, the star wide receiver for the Oakland Raiders, sprints up hills for hours each week during the off-season in preparation for NFL training camp. Not to be outdone, basketball superstar Karl Malone runs in the thin air of the Utah mountains every summer, conditioning his body for the upcoming NBA season. It is no coincidence that these two competitors are widely considered to be the finest conditioned athletes in their respective sports.

Obviously, the hill grade you use will vary depending on the availability of the appropriate landscape. As a rule, steep grades (7- to 10-degree angles) should be utilized for short, explosive sprints, covering ten yards or so. Flatter grades (1.0- to 3.5-degree angles) can be used for sprints ranging from 20 to 80 yards.

Stadium-step running should be approached in the same fashion as uphill running. Most large stadiums have suitable inclines and distances to provide good workouts. High-knee lifts should be employed when running up stadium steps. This procedure will increase the intensity of the workout and lessen your chances of stumbling on the steps. Be sure to maintain full concentration on the decent down the steps in between sprints.

Sand Sprinting

Just as jogging along a scenic beach near the water's edge is an excellent and pleasant way to enhance your level of aerobic conditioning, sprinting on the soft sand 20 feet or so above the shoreline can be an outstanding vehicle for improving speed, explosiveness, balance, lower body strength, and anaerobic conditioning. Many elite athletes from a cross-section of sports make use of sand sprinting on a regular basis.

The distances you sprint in the sand can vary, but for basketball purposes, 10- to 30-yard all-out efforts are most effective. The same rest intervals used in track workouts can be incorporated into your sand-running sessions. Running shoes may be worn, but because sprinting barefoot in the soft sand will strengthen your calves, feet, and ankles to a much greater degree, this technique is highly recommended.

Although running on soft sand is fairly safe, you must take some routine precautions before beginning your workouts. First, carefully check the surface where you're going to be sprinting for broken glass (unfortunately, it is frequently found on beaches these days), large rocks, broken seashells, or any other obstacle that may inhibit your running or cause injury. Second, make sure you are thoroughly warmed up, especially your lower legs. Many athletes sustain injuries running in the sand when they neglect to adequately warm-up. Finally, if you have a history of Achilles-tendon problems or are prone to hamstring pulls, sprinting on sand should be avoided.

I spent many summers sprinting on the beautiful beaches of Long Island, New York, preparing for my upcoming basketball seasons, and found it to be a rewarding and performance enhancing experience. If you're fortunate enough to live near the beach, take my advice and hit the sand for some sprint work.

Boxing

While this book's focus is on basketball training, it is important to expose you to a conditioning method that can enhance both your basketball workouts and your on-court performance. Boxing workouts can be terrific complements to your basketball training sessions. It takes as little as five lessons to become proficient enough to enjoy productive workouts, and most basketball players adjust fairly easily to boxing training. The recommended routines for boxing training involve shadow boxing, footwork drills, rope skipping, abdominal training, hitting heavy and speed bags, and ring work with a trainer. Live sparring is not necessary or suggested for basketball players. Boxing training, especially heavy-bag work, loosens the muscles of your upper body, along with strengthening your arms, shoulders, upper back, hands, and wrists. Your footwork can be improved by skipping rope and by performing in-ring sliding drills. Hand-eye coordination can be enhanced by working the speed bag and by shadow boxing. A boxing workout can also provide both aerobic and anaerobic conditioning benefits. Accordingly, if there is a boxing gym or a health club that offers boxing classes in your area, sign up for some lessons and take advantage of a superb conditioning tool. Table 11-1 presents an overview of a sample boxing workout you can perform.

1 round shadow boxing (warm-up)	2 rounds in-ring footwork drills
1 round rope skipping	2 rounds rope skipping
3 rounds heavy bag work	2 rounds abdominal training
2 rounds speed bag work	1 round shadow boxing (cool-down)

▶ The workout is based on three-minute rounds and one-minute rest intervals between rounds.

▶ Total workout time = 57 minutes

Table 11-1. A sample boxing workout

Fartlek Training

Fartlek training, or "speed play" as it is sometimes called, originated in Sweden and involves running at different speeds for arbitrary intervals of time or distance. The intervals and pace chosen are totally up to the runner. As a rule, approximately 50% jogging and 50% striding/sprinting is suggested for best results. Many conditioning experts feel that fartlek training is tailor-made for basketball players, because it creates an atmosphere of non-planned speed changes similar to a basketball game. The technique also provides substantial aerobic and anaerobic conditioning benefits.

I was originally exposed to fartlek training by legendary Duke University track coach, Al Buehler. Coach Buehler would lead the men's basketball team through Fartlek sessions on the Duke campus golf course, where the chosen running path had the perfect complement of hills, turns, and flat straight-aways. While the golf course was ideal for fartlek training, the workouts can just as easily be executed on a track or around the perimeter of a football or soccer field. For basketball purposes, fartlek workouts should last between 20 and 40 minutes. Table 11-2 illustrates an example of a fartlek training session:

Jog: 5 minutes > **Stride:** 3 minutes > **Jog:** 2 minutes > **Sprint:** 90 seconds >
Jog: 1 minute > **Stride:** 2 minutes > **Sprint:** 1 minute > **Jog:** 3 minutes >
Sprint: 30 seconds > **Stride:** 2 minutes > **Jog:** 2 minutes > **Sprint:** 1 minute >
Stride: 1 minute > **Jog:** 2 minutes > **Sprint:** 90 seconds > **Jog:** 1 minute >
Sprint: 30 seconds > **Jog:** 1 minute

Table 11-2. Sample fartlek training session

Failure Sprinting

The most exhausting form of cross training is discussed last in this chapter. Failure sprinting is not well known in the sports conditioning community—probably because it's so painful to perform. It entails running full speed for as long as your body holds out—no breaks, no let ups, just all-out sprinting until you can't sprint anymore. The distance you cover will depend on your speed, physical conditioning, genetic potential, and most importantly, your ability to handle pain. Notwithstanding its grueling nature, failure sprinting is perhaps the most effective way to train the lactic acid system (refer to chapter 3) and should be incorporated in your anaerobic conditioning program in lieu of conventional sprints from time to time.

Failure sprints are best performed on a long, flat straightaway. If that type of surface is not available to you, sprinting to failure around a track or even performing repetitive-length sprints on a basketball court will do. It is recommended that you begin each failure sprint with 20 to 30 yards of striding. The rest intervals between sets should correlate with the work:rest ratios documented in chapter 5. Depending on your conditioning level, two to four failure sprints per workout are recommended. Failure sprints should only be incorporated after you have performed four to five weeks of sprint workouts.

FULL-YEAR STRENGTH AND CONDITIONING CALENDAR

JANUARY

Sun	Mon	Tue	Wed	Thu	Fri	Sat
				1 Practice Strength Train Workout #1	**2** Practice	**3** Game (afternoon)
4 Strength Train Workout #2	**5** Practice	**6** Game (night)	**7** Practice Strength Train Workout #1	**8** Practice	**9** Practice	**10** Game (afternoon) Strength Train Workout #2
11 Rest	**12** Practice Strength Train Workout #1	**13** Practice	**14** Game (night)	**15** Practice	**16** Game (night)	**17** Rest
18 Strength Train Workout #2	**19** Practice	**20** Practice	**21** Game (night)	**22** Practice Strength Train Workout #1	**23** Practice	**24** Practice
25 Strength Train Workout #2	**26** Practice	**27** Game (night)	**28** Strength Train Workout #1	**29** Practice	**30** Practice	**31** Game (afternoon)

FEBRUARY

Sun	Mon	Tue	Wed	Thu	Fri	Sat
1 Strength Train Workout #2	**2** Practice	**3** Practice	**4** Game (night)	**5** Practice Strength Train Workout #1	**6** Practice	**7** Game (afternoon) Strength Train Workout #2
8 Rest	**9** Practice Strength Train Workout #1	**10** Practice	**11** Game (night)	**12** Strength Train Workout #2	**13** Practice	**14** Game (afternoon)
15 Strength Train Workout #1	**16** Practice	**17** Practice	**18** Game (night)	**19** Practice Strength Train Workout #2	**20** Practice	**21** Game (afternoon)
22 Strength Train Workout #1	**23** Practice	**24** Game (night)	**25** Rest	**26** Practice Strength Train Workout #2	**27** Practice	**28** Game (night)

MARCH

Sun	Mon	Tue	Wed	Thu	Fri	Sat
1 Rest	**2** Practice Strength Train Workout #1	**3** Practice	**4** Practice Strength Train Workout #2	**5** Practice	**6** Conference Tournament	**7** Conference Tournament
8 Conference Tournament	**9** Strength Train Workout #1	**10** Practice	**11** Practice Strength Train Workout #2	**12** Practice	**13** NCAA Tournament 1st Round	**14** Practice
15 NCAA Tournament 2nd Round	**16** Strength Train Workout #1	**17** Practice	**18** Practice Strength Train Workout #2	**19** Practice	**20** NCAA Tournament 3rd Round	**21** Practice
22 NCAA Tournament Quarterfinals	**23** Rest	**24** Practice Strength Train Workout #1	**25** Practice	**26** Practice	**27** Practice	**28** NCAA Tournament Semifinals
29 Practice	**30** NCAA Tournament Finals	**31** Rest				

APRIL

Sun	Mon	Tue	Wed	Thu	Fri	Sat
		1 Rest	**2** Rest	**3** Rest	**4** Rest	**5** Rest
6 Rest	**7** Rest	**8** Rest	**9** Rest	**10** Rest	**11** Rest	**12** Rest
13 Rest	**14** Aerobic Conditioning	**15** Off-Season Mini-Cycle 1 Strength Train Workout #1	**16**	**17** Strength Train Workout #2	**18** Aerobic Conditioning	**19** Strength Train Workout #1
20 Aerobic Conditioning	**21** Strength Train Workout #2	**22** Aerobic Conditioning	**23**	**24** Strength Train Workout #1	**25** Aerobic Conditioning	**26** Strength Train Workout #2
27 Aerobic Conditioning	**28** Strength Train Workout #1	**29** Aerobic Conditioning	**30** Strength Train Workout #2			

MAY

Sun	Mon	Tue	Wed	Thu	Fri	Sat
				1	2 Aerobic Conditioning	3 Strength Train Workout #1
4 Aerobic Conditioning	5 Strength Train Workout #2	6 Aerobic Conditioning	7 Strength Train Workout #1	8	9 Strength Train Workout #2	10 Aerobic Conditioning
11	12 Aerobic Conditioning Strength Train Workout #1	13	14 Aerobic Conditioning Strength Train Workout #2	15 Aerobic Conditioning	16 Off-Season Mini-Cycle 2 Strength Train Workout #1	17 Aerobic Conditioning
18 Strength Train Workout #2	19 Aerobic Conditioning	20 Aerobic Conditioning Strength Train Workout #1	21	22 Aerobic Conditioning Strength Train Workout #2	23	24 Aerobic Conditioning
25 Strength Train Workout #1	26 Strength Train Workout #2	27 Aerobic/ Anaerobic Combination	28 Strength Train Workout #1	29	30 Aerobic/ Anaerobic Combination	31 Strength Train Workout #2

JUNE

Sun	Mon	Tue	Wed	Thu	Fri	Sat
1	2 Strength Train Workout #1	3 Aerobic/ Anaerobic Combination	4	5 Strength Train Workout #2	6 Aerobic/ Anaerobic Combination	7 Strength Train Workout #1
8	9 Strength Train Workout #2	10	11 Strength Train Workout #1	12	13	14 Strength Train Workout #2
15 Strength Train Workout #1	16	17 Anaerobic Conditioning Strength Train Workout #2	18	19 Strength Train Workout #1	20 Anaerobic Conditioning	21 Strength Train Workout #2
22	23 Strength Train Workout #1	24	25 Anaerobic Conditioning	26	27	28 Anaerobic Conditioning
29	30					

JULY

Sun	Mon	Tue	Wed	Thu	Fri	Sat
		1 Anaerobic Conditioning Off-Season Mini-Cycle 3 Strength Train Workout #2	**2**	**3** Strength Train Workout #1	**4** Anaerobic Conditioning	**5** Strength Train Workout #2
6	**7** Strength Train Workout #1	**8**	**9** Anaerobic Conditioning	**10** Strength Train Workout #2	**11**	**12** Anaerobic Conditioning Strength Train Workout #1
13	**14** Strength Train Workout #2	**15** Anaerobic Conditioning	**16** Strength Train Workout #1	**17**	**18** Anaerobic Conditioning	**19** Strength Train Workout #2
20 Strength Train Workout #1	**21** Plyometrics/ Agility	**22** Strength Train Workout #2	**23** Anaerobic Conditioning	**24** Strength Train Workout #1	**25** Plyometrics/ Agility	**26** Anaerobic Conditioning
27 Strength Train Workout #2	**28** Plyometrics/ Agility	**29** Anaerobic Conditioning Strength Train Workout #1	**30**	**31** Strength Train Workout #2		

AUGUST

Sun	Mon	Tue	Wed	Thu	Fri	Sat
					1 Anaerobic Conditioning	**2** Plyometrics/ Agility Strength Train Workout #1
3	**4** Strength Train Workout #2	**5** Plyometrics/ Agility	**6** Anaerobic Conditioning	**7** Strength Train Workout #1	**8** Plyometrics/ Agility Strength Train Workout #2	**9** Anaerobic Conditioning
10	**11** Plyometrics/ Agility	**12** Anaerobic Conditioning	**13**	**14**	**15** Anaerobic Conditioning Pre-Season Mini-Cycle 1 Strength Train Workout #1	**16** Plyometrics/ Agility
17 Strength Train Workout #2	**18** Plyometrics/ Agility	**19** Strength Train Workout #1	**20**	**21** Strength Train Workout #2	**22** Plyometrics/ Agility	**23**
24 Strength Train Workout #1 **31**	**25** Plyometrics/ Agility	**26** Strength Train Workout #2	**27** Anaerobic Conditioning	**28** Strength Train Workout #1	**29** Plyometrics/ Agility	**30** Anaerobic Conditioning Strength Train Workout #2

SEPTEMBER

Sun	Mon	Tue	Wed	Thu	Fri	Sat
	1 Plyometrics/ Agility	**2** Anaerobic Conditioning Strength Train Workout #1	**3**	**4** Strength Train Workout #2	**5** Anaerobic Conditioning	**6** Plyometrics/ Agility Strength Train Workout #1
7	**8** Strength Train Workout #2	**9** Plyometrics/ Agility	**10** Anaerobic Conditioning	**11** Strength Train Workout #1	**12** Plyometrics/ Agility	**13** Anaerobic Conditioning Strength Train Workout #2
14 Plyometrics/ Agility	**15** Strength Train Workout #1	**16** Anaerobic Conditioning	**17** Strength Train Workout #2	**18** Plyometrics/ Agility	**19** Anaerobic Conditioning Strength Train Workout #1	**20**
21 Strength Train Workout #2	**22** Plyometrics/ Agility	**23** Strength Train Workout #1	**24**	**25** Strength Train Workout #2	**26** Plyometrics/ Agility	**27** Strength Train Workout #1
28	**29** Plyometrics/ Agility	**30** Pre-Season Mini-Cycle 2 Strength Train Workout #2	**31**			

OCTOBER

Sun	Mon	Tue	Wed	Thu	Fri	Sat
			1	2 Strength Train Workout #1	3 Plyometrics/ Agility	4 Strength Train Workout #2
5	6 Strength Train Workout #1	7 Plyometrics/ Agility	8 Strength Train Workout #2	9	10 Strength Train Workout #1	11 Plyometrics/ Agility
12 Strength Train Workout #2	13 Rest	14 Rest	15 Practice Begins Practice	16 In-Season Mini-Cycle 1 Practice Strength Train Workout #1	17 Practice	18 Practice Strength Train Workout #2
19	20 Practice	21 Practice Strength Train Workout #1	22 Practice Strength Train Workout #2	23 Practice	24 Practice Strength Train Workout #1	25 Rest
26 Intra-Squad Scrimmage (night)	27 Strength Train Workout #2	28 Practice	29 Practice Strength Train Workout #1	30 Practice	31 Practice Strength Train Workout #2	

NOVEMBER

Sun	Mon	Tue	Wed	Thu	Fri	Sat
						1 Practice
2 Strength Train Workout #1	**3** Practice	**4** Rest	**5** Practice Strength Train Workout #2	**6** Practice	**7** Practice Strength Train Workout #1	**8** Practice
9 Strength Train Workout #2	**10** Practice	**11** Exhibition Game (night)	**12** Rest	**13** Practice Strength Train Workout #1	**14** Practice	**15** Practice
16 In-Season Mini-Cycle 2 Strength Train Workout #2	**17** Practice	**18** Practice	**19** Game (night)	**20** Practice Strength Train Workout #1	**21** Practice	**22** Game (night)
23 Game (night) **30** Practice	**24** Rest	**25** Practice Strength Train Workout #2	**26** Practice	**27** Rest (Thanksgiving)	**28** Practice	**29** Game (night) Strength Train Workout #2

DECEMBER

Sun	Mon	Tue	Wed	Thu	Fri	Sat
	1 Game (night)	**2** Rest	**3** Practice Strength Train Workout #1	**4** Practice	**5** Practice	**6** Game (night) Strength Train Workout #2
7 Rest	**8** Practice Strength Train Workout #1	**9** Practice	**10** Practice	**11** Strength Train Workout #2	**12** Practice	**13** Practice
14 Strength Train Workout #1	**15** Practice	**16** Game (night)	**17** Practice	**18** Game (night)	**19** Strength Train Workout #2	**20** Rest
21 Practice Strength Train Workout #1	**22** Practice	**23** Practice Strength Train Workout #2	**24** Practice	**25** Rest	**26** Practice	**27** Game (afternoon) Strength Train Workout #1
28 Rest	**29** Practice Strength Train Workout #2	**30** Practice	**31** Game (night)			

ABOUT THE AUTHOR

Tom Emma is the president of Power Performance, Inc., a company that specializes in training athletes in strength, conditioning, and athletic enhancement techniques. He is a graduate of Duke University, where he was a three-year starter on the basketball team and squad captain his senior year. His .843 career free-throw percentage is among the highest in Duke history. He was drafted by the Chicago Bulls in the 1983 NBA draft. Tom has a masters degree from Columbia University and lives in New York City.